SADLIER
FAITH AND
WITNESS

CREED

A Course on Catholic Belief

Norman F. Josaitis, S.T.D.

Rev. Michael J. Lanning, O.F.M.

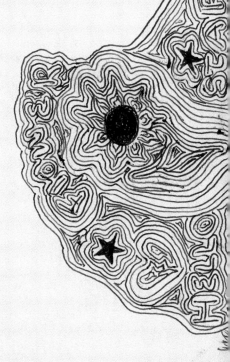

William H. Sadlier, Inc.
9 Pine Street
New York, New York 10005-1002

Acknowledgments

Scripture selections are taken from the *New American Bible* ©1991, 1986, 1970 by the Confraternity of Christian Doctrine, Washington, D.C. and are used with permission. All rights reserved.

Excerpts from the English translation of the *Catechism of the Catholic Church* for use in the United States of America, ©1994, United States Catholic Conference, Inc.—Libreria Editrice Vaticana. Used with permission.

Excerpts from the English translation of The *Roman Missal* ©1973, International Committee on English in the Liturgy, Inc. (ICEL); the English translation of the Act of Contrition from the *Rite of Penance* ©1974, ICEL; the English translation of the Hail, Holy Queen, the Angelus, the Prayer for Unity, and the Prayer to the Holy Spirit from *A Book of Prayers* ©1982, ICEL; the English translation of May the Angels from the *Order of Christian Funerals* ©1985, ICEL. All rights reserved.

English translation of the Our Father, Apostles' Creed, and Nicene Creed by the International Consultation on English Texts, (ICET).

Act of Faith, Act of Hope, Act of Love from *Handbook for Today's Catholic* ©1994, Liguori Publications, are used with permission. All rights reserved.

The Mysteries of the Rosary, *Catholic Household Blessings and Prayers* © 1988 United States Catholic Conference, Washington, D.C. Used with permission.

Excerpt from *Crossing the Threshold of Hope* by His Holiness Pope John Paul II, translation ©1994 by Alfred A. Knopf, Inc. Reprinted by permission of Random House, Inc.

Excerpts from *The Documents of Vatican II*, Walter M. Abbott, S.J., General Editor, ©1966 by America Press, Inc. Used with permission.

Cover Illustrator: Diane Fenster

Photo Credits

Jim Saylor   Mary Kate Coudal
Photo Editor   *Photo Researcher*

Cover Photos

Art Resource: back cover, center. *The Crosiers/* Gene Plaisted, OSC: front cover, bottom left; front cover, top right. *Anne Hamersky:* back cover, top left.

Photo Credits

ABC Studios: 154 left. *Adventure Photo and Film:* 33; Pressenbild: 36; Steven Alvarez: 49; Michael Powers: 105; Barbara Brown: 175 bottom. *Animals Animals/* E.R. Degginger: 112–113. *Art Resource:* 114; Erich Lessing: 6 right, 79, 160–161; Scala: 59, 80; Giraudon: 92. *John Brandi Jr.:* 84. *Kevin Butler:* 22–23, 103, 140–141, 174–175. *Myrleen Cate:* 55. *Catholic News Service:* 143; Lisa Kessler: 34; Bob Roller: 141 bottom; Michael Edrington: 175 top. *Dwight Cendrowski:* 154 right. *Cleo Photography:* 82. *Carr Clifton:* 73. *Comstock:* 97, 124–125 basilica. *Corbis:* 84–85. *The Crosiers/* Gene Plaisted, OSC: 22, 23, 96, 119, 141 top, 142, 144 right, 154 bottom, 167, 168 all, 169. *Leo de Wys/* Sipa: 106–107 statue, 124–125 hands; Riclafe: 182–183. *Don Eastman:* 109 top. *Envision, Inc./* Norman Isaacs: 16–17. *FPG/* Joseph Beck: 10 bottom right; Jean Kugler: 12 left; Michael Hart: 19 left; Andrea Sperling: 42; Telegraph Colour Library: 66; Ron Thomas: 68; Arthur Tilley: 83 left; Toyohiro Yamada: 90; Bob Peterson: 164. *Robert Fried:* 72. *The Glasgow Museum:* 94. *The Granger Collection:* 8 top, 9, 10 top. *Anne Hamersky:* 56. *Benedictine Sisters of Perpetual Adoration:* 152 top. *Bob Hand:* 61. *The Image Bank/* Maria Taglienti: 19 right; Steven Hunt: 40–41; Eric Meola: 45 bottom; Alberto Inrocci: 67; Ira Block: 69; G&M David de Lossy: 71 top; Simon Wilkinson: 76–77; Frank Wise: 83 right; Grant Faint: 166; Alexander Stewart: 180–181. *L'osservatore Romano/Catholic Near East Magazine:* 156.

Liaison International/ J&M Studios: 32; James Schnepf: 35 top; Douglas Burrows: 35 bottom; Lien/Nebauer: 43 bottom; Larry Mayer: 54; Michael Renaudeau: 70–71; Sheila Beougher: 126 center; Noel: 133 top; F. Lo Chon: 133 bottom; A. Georgeon: 153; Anticoli Luvio: 172–173. *Ken Karp:* 144 left. *The Metropolitan Museum of Art/* Gift of Mrs. Myron C. Taylor, 1938: 10 bottom left. *Steve Moriarity:* 88–89. *Palm Beach Post/* John Lopinot: 120–121; Loren Hosack: 127. *Richard Pasley:* 44 top. *Photo Edit/* Alan Oddie: 104. *Photonica/* Kazuyuki Hashimoto: 129; Mel Curtis: 162–163. *Picture Perfect:* 121 top; K. Schlea: 116. *Frances Roberts:* 120–121. *Chris Sheridan:* 145, 152 bottom, 181. *Dana Sigall:* 91. *Stock Imagery/* Kaiser: 130. *Stock Market/* Tom Sanders: 31; Zefa/Mael: 44 center; Mugshots: 46; Stocknet: 100–101; Peter Steiner: 117; Bilderberg: 138. *Superstock:* 37, 64–65, 81; Kris Coppieters: 176. *Tony Stone Images:* 92–93, 126 background; Olaf Soot: 4–5; Hugh Sitton: 6 center; Tom Till: 6–7; Robert Evans: 8–9; Peter Wilkie: 11 right; Hideo Kurihara: 12 right; Paul Chesley: 13; David Young Wolff: 19 top; David Hiser: 20; John Lund: 28–29; Thomas Brase: 30; Chad Slattery: 43 top; World Prospective: 47; Glen Allison: 52–53; Bruce Ayres: 57; Mitch Kezar: 60; David Higgs: 70 top; Barbara Filet: 70 bottom; Laurence Dutton: 71 bottom; Richard Passmore: 78; Darrell Gulin: 82–83; Rich Frishman: 109 bottom; Bob Daemmrich: 121 bottom; Brian Bailey: 150; Vera Storman: 165; Patricia Thompson: 177. *Jacqueline Srouji:* 141 center. *SYGMA/* G. Giansanti: 136–137, 148–149. *Larry Ulrich:* 102. *Unicorn/* Jeff Greenberg: 120. *Uniphoto:* 24, 48, 115. *Viesti Associates, Inc.:* 21; Joe Viesti: 11 left. *Westlight/* Bill Lisenby: 106–107 statue.

General Consultant
Rev. Joseph A. Komonchak, Ph.D.

Official Theological Consultant
Most Rev. Edward K. Braxton, Ph.D., S.T.D.
Auxiliary Bishop of St. Louis

Publisher
Gerard F. Baumbach, Ed.D.

Editor in Chief
Moya Gullage

Pastoral Consultant
Rev. Msgr. John F. Barry

Scriptural Consultant
Rev. Donald Senior, C.P., Ph.D., S.T.D.

General Editors
Norman F. Josaitis, S.T.D.
Rev. Michael J. Lanning, O.F.M.

Catechetical and Liturgical Consultants
Eleanor Ann Brownell, D. Min.
Joseph F. Sweeney
Helen Hemmer, I.H.M.
Mary Frances Hession
Maureen Sullivan, O.P., Ph.D.
Don Boyd

"The Ad Hoc Committee to Oversee the Use of the Catechism,
National Conference of Catholic Bishops,
has found this catechetical text to be in conformity
with the *Catechism of the Catholic Church*."

Nihil Obstat
✠ Most Reverend George O. Wirz
Censor Librorum

Imprimatur
✠ Most Reverend William H. Bullock
Bishop of Madison
April 25, 1997

The *Nihil Obstat* and *Imprimatur* are official
declarations that a book or pamphlet is free of
doctrinal or moral error. No implication is contained
therein that those who have granted the *Nihil Obstat*
and *Imprimatur* agree with the contents, opinions, or
statements expressed.

Printed in the United States of America.

S is a registered trademark of William H. Sadlier, Inc.

Home Office:
9 Pine Street
New York, NY 10005–1002

ISBN: 8215-5602-9
123456789/987

THE AMAZING SEARCH FOR GOD

Praise the LORD, all you nations!
Give glory, all you peoples!

Psalm 117:1

NO matter where you go, you will always find the influence of religion. Whether you stay in your hometown or travel around the globe, you will always find it. In fact some of the world's most beautiful structures were built because of religion and the search for God. Why is this so? How would you explain it?

*Stonehenge in England and
Moai stone statues on Easter Island*

The Search Begins

Our Catholic faith gives us the answer to these questions: "The desire for God is written in the human heart" because we were created by God and for God (*Catechism of the Catholic Church, 27*). What does this mean? It means that the search for God is a part of being human. And it has been that way from the beginning.

Did all people find the one true God in their search? Did everyone discover the truth about God? Let's take a look. As we do, we will begin to realize even more that being a Catholic is something very special.

Even before the dawn of history, primitive people were searching for God. When they looked far into the night sky and saw the moon and the stars, what did they think of those shining lights? When a baby was born or someone died, what thoughts raced through their minds? Where did the world around them come from? Who or what kept the stars in their places?

Studies of prehistoric times give clues that can help us answer these questions. When the dwelling places of ancient peoples are unearthed, they tell us many things about the way these people lived and thought—even what they thought about life and death. The burial places of these ancient peoples are filled with articles from everyday life, such as jewelry, tools, and weapons. All these items would be needed in the life they looked forward to after death.

In addition people were frequently buried with offerings for their gods. Sometimes small idols of gods have been found. Close to primitive dwellings and burial places, we also find the remains of altars, temples, and other items of worship. Clearly the ancients did not think they were alone in the universe.

All the evidence that modern men and women have discovered points to the fact that most, if not all, ancient peoples had their own ideas of a god or gods and their own practice of a religion. It seems that some form of religious expression has been part of human experience from the beginning.

Today we know that the practice of religion is universal. It is found all over the world. If you travel to any part of the globe, you will find people practicing a religion of one kind or another. If you look at any period of history, you will discover human beings engaged in religious activities. Among these we find worship of a god or gods, rituals and sacrifices, prayers and meditations, beliefs and doctrines, festivals and pilgrimages.

Religions have used a wide range of ideas to describe their gods or divine powers. Some peoples have worshiped gods that took the form of humans or animals. Some divine powers were identified with the earth or with a mysterious mountain in a region. Other gods were divinities of the sky or of the changing weather or seasons. Still others were believed to be supreme creators or mysterious powers that ran through all of life. How amazing is the human ability to describe and to name what is sacred and divine. It has known no bounds. In fact we can say that of all the creatures on earth human beings are the only religious creatures and that religion has always been an important part of the human story.

This chapter's short survey of some of the world's great religions will highlight the desire for God written in the human heart. It will also challenge us to see how much we know about the uniqueness and beauty of our Catholic faith.

Give one example from your own experience to show that the influence of religion is everywhere.

The Religions of Ancient Greece and Rome

The search for God can be seen in ancient religions. Two of the best known of these religions no longer exist. Nevertheless we know a great deal about them, and they help to shape our language and culture even today. These are the religions of ancient Greece and Rome.

In the ancient Greek and Roman civilizations, it was common to believe in many gods and goddesses. The belief in many gods is called *polytheism*. This is very different from our belief. As Christians we know that there is only one God. Belief in one god is called *monotheism*.

Like many other peoples, the people of ancient Greece believed that their gods were part of the natural world. They thought that gods could live in the sun or the moon or the stars, in running water, in stones or trees, or on sacred mountains. In fact Mount Olympus, the highest mountain in Greece, was regarded as the home of the gods.

The Greek gods and goddesses were thought of as mortal men and women. They could make mistakes, change their minds, be loving or angry. They often were jealous and took revenge on one another. These gods could be either harmful or friendly to human beings. If people did not offer the right sacrifice, they might find themselves in trouble with a god or goddess and suffer the consequences, or so the

ancient Greeks thought. But more often than not, these gods were considered to be friendly. They brought the gifts of food, sunshine, and rain.

Among the many divinities in Greece, the chief god was Zeus, the father and king of the gods and the god of the sky. He ruled on Mount Olympus, the site of his throne. There the gods ate, drank, played, and quarreled with one another, just like human beings. Zeus's wife was the goddess Hera, the queen of the gods.

Zeus's brothers were Poseidon and Hades. Poseidon was the god of the sea and lived in a golden palace far beneath the surface of the water. Hades was the god of the underworld, the place of the dead. The ancient Greeks believed that the souls of the dead were ferried across the river Styx to the underworld. They even had to pay the ferryman Charon to take them across the river.

Head of Zeus

Delphi in Greece

One of the gods was called Apollo. He was the sun god whose fiery chariot lit up the sky each day. He was thought to be so powerful that people would go to his shrine at Delphi to have their questions answered. Their questions were put to a priestess of Apollo at his shrine, and her answers to the questions were supposed to be those of the god himself. Hermes was the messenger of the gods and was pictured as having wings on his feet and wearing a wide-brimmed helmet.

One of Zeus's daughters was called Athena. She was the goddess of wisdom and crafts and patroness of towns and cities. The ancient Greeks pictured her as a beautiful woman dressed in armor who protected them. The modern capital of Greece is called Athens in her honor.

The gods and goddesses of ancient Greece were taken over by the ancient Romans and made a part of their religion. The Romans changed the names of the gods to fit their language, which was Latin. Thus, Zeus became Jupiter, Hera became Juno, and Hermes became Mercury.

These ancient religions may seem far removed from our modern culture. But they were the way the ancient Greeks and Romans searched for God. It may even come as a surprise to many that these ancient religions affect our lives today. For example, the names of the Greek and Roman gods are the names we use for rockets, the months of the year, and the planets of our solar system.

When the planets were first discovered, why do you think they were given the names of Greek and Roman gods?

Statue of Athena

Major Gods of Ancient Greece and Rome

Greek Name	Roman Name	Description
Ares	Mars	god of war
Aphrodite	Venus	goddess of love and beauty
Athena	Minerva	goddess of wisdom
Dionysus	Bacchus	god of crops, fruit, and wine
Hades	Pluto	god of the underworld
Hephaestus	Vulcan	god of fire
Hera	Juno	wife of Zeus, queen of the gods
Hermes	Mercury	messenger of the gods
Poseidon	Neptune	god of the sea
Zeus	Jupiter	father and king of the gods

CATHOLIC ID

One of the best-sellers of the 1990s, *Crossing the Threshold of Hope*, was written by Pope John Paul II. In one of its chapters he dealt with the many religions of the world. He said, "Christ came into the world for all these peoples. He redeemed them all and has His own ways of reaching each of them."

The Religion of Ancient Egypt

Another ancient religion that no longer exists was that of Egypt. Egyptian civilization revolved around the desert and the river Nile. Its religion explained the world in a different way from that of the Greeks and Romans, but it, too, had many gods and goddesses.

Egypt's very life as a nation depended upon the daily appearance of the sun and the annual flooding of the Nile. These events assured that there would be enough food to feed the people. It is no wonder, then, that the gods of ancient Egypt represented the forces of nature. Re was the sun god. He was considered the king of the gods. Osiris, the god of vegetation, was equally important, as was his wife, Isis, known as the queen of the gods.

Ancient Egypt cannot be separated from its religion. Its world and the world of the gods were considered as one. Thus, the gods could be pictured as creatures that were half human and half animal. And human beings were destined for an afterlife cared for by the gods.

People believed they would be judged by the way they lived. At death a person's heart was weighed in a balance. Anubis, the god of the dead, led the soul to judgment. The soul lived on, but it somehow needed the physical body for survival. That is why the bodies of the dead were treated with preservatives and dried out, a process called mummification.

Today the pyramids of Egypt, the mummies, and the other objects we see in museums are lasting reminders of the ancient Egyptians and their religious beliefs.

 Have you ever seen a mummy? Describe the experience.

Statue of Anubis (left); Osiris seated on a throne (above); pyramids at Giza

Woman with sacred cow and statue of Hindu deities

Hinduism

Hinduism, the oldest religion in the world, is practiced by more than 700 million people today. Its traditions go back five thousand years. Like the ancient Egyptian religion, Hinduism had no single founder. It is generally associated with one country, India. In fact the word *Hindu* means "one from India."

The beliefs of modern Hindus flow from the Vedas ("knowledge"), their sacred writings of hymns and prayers to the gods. Hindu beliefs are also found in the famous Bhagavad Gita ("Song of the Lord"), the best-known devotional literature of Hinduism. Hindu beliefs center on the ideas of Brahman, reincarnation, and salvation.

Brahman is the divine source of all life, a divine power. However, it is unknowable to human beings. That is why there are many gods; they are the expressions of Brahman. Nevertheless Hindus do not consider themselves polytheists because Brahman is the one source of all.

Hindus believe in reincarnation, also known as transmigration of souls. Reincarnation means that when people die, their souls return to earth and are rejoined to another body. This process of reincarnation goes on endlessly until one is able to break the cycle and become one with Brahman. Salvation means being liberated from this endless cycle of rebirths. It is achieved by self-control, living a good life, and developing a sincere devotion to a god. In the end a soul can come to rest only through oneness with Brahman. This is the goal of one's life, and all things should contribute to this goal.

In Hinduism the cycle of life is closely tied with the sacred river Ganges in India. At death Hindus are cremated, and their ashes are sprinkled into this river to be part of the flow of life. The water of this sacred river becomes a symbol of life without end, going on and on.

There are many Hindu temples in which prayers and sacrifices are offered to the gods. The Hindu priests who perform the temple ceremonies are called brahmins. But prayer and worship are not confined to temples. Many Hindus have shrines or pictures of their gods in their homes. The home and nature itself are places and sources of ritual and devotion. That is the reason cows are sacred to Hindus; cows are the symbols of Mother Earth and the wonderful gifts that we receive from the earth.

For millions of people Hinduism is a way of life. It is one of the world's great religions, and it influences the way its members look at the world.

Scripture UPDATE

People frequently think of the Bible in terms of Jews and Christians. As a matter of fact, however, the first eleven chapters of the Bible are about all of humanity before Abraham—before any distinctions were made among different types of people. Even the New Testament praises many of these people for their holiness. In Hebrews 11:4, for example, Abel, a son of Adam and Eve, is praised for the sacrifice he offered to God.

Image of Buddha and Buddhist temple

Buddhism

Another world religion practiced by millions today began as a reform movement in Hinduism. Its founder was Siddhartha Gautama, born in India of a royal family around 560 B.C. Gautama was dissatisfied with the answers to life that were given by Hinduism, and he began to search for a new understanding of life and salvation.

It was only after a long and difficult search that Gautama felt he was enlightened and had discovered the answers to his questions. For this reason his followers called him the *Buddha*, a title meaning "the enlightened one." After his enlightenment the Buddha traveled for forty-four years throughout India. He lived as a beggar monk, gathering many disciples around him and teaching the way of enlightenment that he had come to know in his life.

Gautama no longer preached the Hindu doctrine that Brahman was the source and end of life. Rather he stressed the fact that individuals play the main part in their salvation. He continued, however, to teach the idea of reincarnation, along with a strong code of moral behavior that stressed noble thoughts, words, and deeds.

Some Buddhists today consider Buddha to be the incarnation of a god. His teachings are written down and are held to be the Buddhist scriptures. Although Buddhism was born in India, it has become a principal religion, not of India, but of the rest of Asia.

Try to find out how many people practice Buddhism and in what countries they live. Share what you find out.

CATHOLIC TEACHINGS

About Other Religions

The Second Vatican Council (1962–1965) stated, "Other religions to be found everywhere strive variously to answer the restless searchings of the human heart.... The Catholic Church rejects nothing which is true and holy in these religions." *Non-Christian Religions, 2*

Islam

The youngest of the great world religions, Islam originated in the early seventh century A.D. in Arabia, today called Saudi Arabia. *Islam* means "surrender"; and the followers of Islam are called *Muslims*, meaning "those who surrender to God."

Muhammad, the founder of Islam, was born in the city of Mecca about A.D. 570. As a young man he followed the polytheistic religion of his homeland, but he was acquainted with Judaism and Christianity. Later in his life Muhammad felt called by God to proclaim a strict monotheism. He urged people to surrender their whole lives to the one and only God. The Arabic word for God is *Allah*. The profession of faith for every Muslim, therefore, is that there is only one God, Allah, and that Muhammad is his prophet.

Islam spread rapidly to millions of people. Its teachings are contained in the holy book, or scriptures, called the Qur'an. For Muslims Friday is the day reserved each week for common worship. However, each Muslim is called to pray five times daily: at daybreak, noon, midafternoon, sunset, and nighttime. In Muslim countries the call to prayer is given from the minaret, a tall tower at the side of a mosque, the Muslim house of worship. These daily prayers can be said either in private or with others and are always said facing Mecca. The prayer ritual includes bowing until the person is on his or her knees with forehead touching the floor. This prayer action symbolizes the total submission of a person to God.

Other duties of Islam include almsgiving for the poor and needy; fasting, especially during the month of Ramadan; and making a pilgrimage to Mecca once in a lifetime, if possible. Through their prayers and other religious practices, Muslims show the world their submission to Allah.

A Whole New Way

The search for God has taken many different paths. Now we know why the Church teaches that the desire for God is written in the human heart. But how do we as Catholics fit into this search for God? Where are our roots, and why are we so different?

About three thousand years ago, a new religion, the religion of the Israelites, was born. It began with one individual who was invited by the one true God into a new relationship such as the world had never known. This individual was Abraham. No longer would he worship many gods. Now he knew that there was only one God. Abraham and his family risked everything to follow God's invitation. Abraham did not know where it would lead. All he knew was that this God, who was calling him, was like no other.

From this divine invitation and Abraham's response, there eventually emerged two of the world's great religions: Judaism and Christianity. What made these religions so special? What set them apart from all the other religions of the world? The answer to these questions can be found in one word: revelation. Because it is such an important idea, all of Chapter 2 will be about revelation.

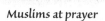

Muslims at prayer

things to think about

What differences do you note among the many religions you have just studied?

What similarities do you detect?

Do you think that knowing about other religions can help you to understand your own religion better?

things to share

Which of the religions discussed in this chapter would you like to know more about?

Team up with others who share your interest. Look up information about that religion or talk with someone who practices it. Let others know how much you respect the many wonders of the human religious experience.

WORDS TO REMEMBER

Find and define the following:

polytheism _____

_____

_____

monotheism _____

_____

_____

OnLine

WITH THE PARISH

Now that you know what the Church teaches about other religions, work with a liturgy-planning team in your parish and together make up some petitions for the Prayer of the Faithful. You might pray that people will show respect for all religions and that everyone will be brought to a greater knowledge and love of God.

Explain this statement: The desire for God is written in the human heart.

It means that the search for God is a part of being human.

Name two religions that no longer exist. Choose one of their beliefs and explain it in your own words.

Greece and Rome
the Greek religion is a polytheism religion. this means that they belive in many god and goddesses and afterlife

Why do Hindus think of themselves as monotheists rather than polytheists?

Because they belive in only one god like us.

What is your understanding of the Hindu and Buddhist belief in reincarnation?

they belive that when you die you come back as another creature.

Describe the daily prayer practices of Muslims.

they wake up and go to pray then they go back to daily life then the pray then they pray, then at midafternoon, and sunset and finally at nighttime.

Life in the Spirit

Go to a quiet space where you can explore your past. Look for clues in your childhood. What evidence can you find that God was in your life? Did you sense that Someone loved you even before you were born and would go on loving you after you died? Did you feel God's presence in your parents' arms and in the laughter of a friend? Did you feel like saying, "Awesome! Nice work, God!" when you saw a mountain or smelled the sea? Pray with all who believe in God:

The LORD is true God,
   he is the living God, the
      eternal King.
Jeremiah 10:10

A Divine and Awesome Invitation

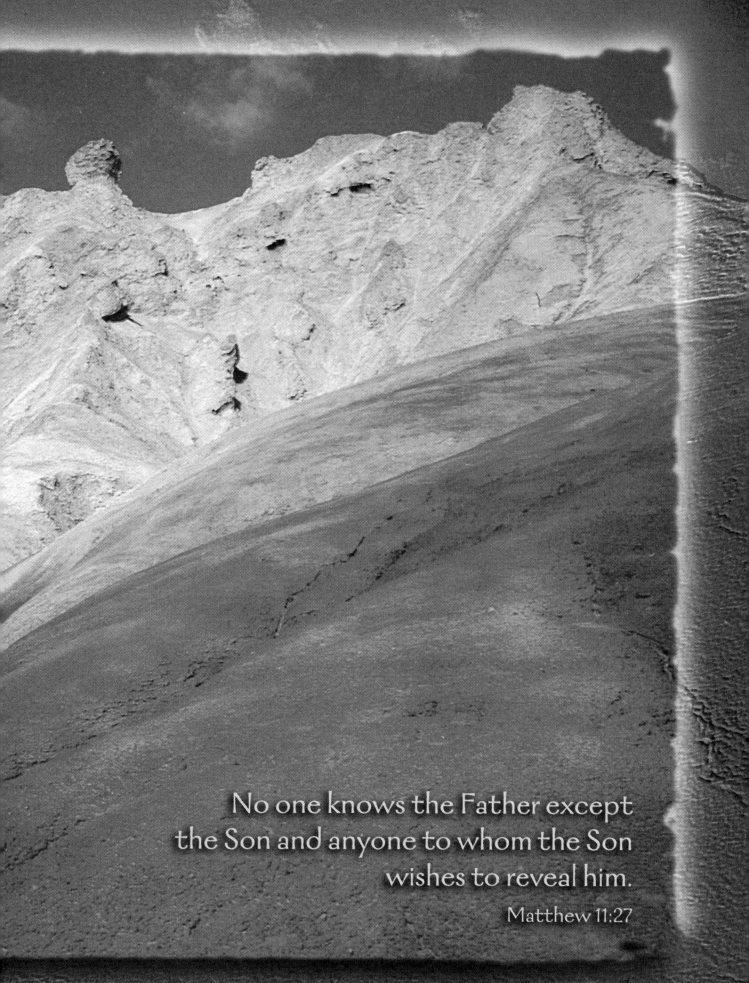

CHAPTER 2

No one knows the Father except
the Son and anyone to whom the Son
wishes to reveal him.

Matthew 11:27

HOW do you really get to know someone?
How do you let others know about yourself,
about what you are thinking and feeling?

Getting to Know Someone

It may sound strange, but we can live next door to people and never really get to know them. Why is this so? Perhaps they are shy or speak a different language. Maybe they attend a different school or place of worship. It could be that we have never invited them to know us. Whatever the reason may be, all we can say about these neighbors is what we see or what others have told us about them. The only way we can really know them is if they tell us about themselves.

When people make themselves known to us and tell us who they are, we say that they reveal themselves to us. When this happens, we really get to know them for the first time. Take, for example, popular singers or sports figures we admire. We listen to their music or perhaps watch every game they play, but we may never know anything about their personal lives or beliefs. These will remain unknown to us unless we meet the people we admire face-to-face or find out, through TV or magazine interviews, what they have to say about themselves.

Getting to Know God

Once we understand the way we get to know someone, we are getting close to knowing the meaning of revelation. Revelation is the act of a person. It is the opening up of one person to another. What does this have to do with God? It is what God has done. God has opened himself to us and has let us know his deepest Self.

Of course, even before any special act of revelation, God had already left his "footprints" in creation. Along with all other peoples, we see God's footprints in the wonders of our universe. God is like a great artist who can be recognized in his work. But we cannot know God as he really is unless he tells us more about himself, unless God reveals himself to us.

You may wish to read part of Abraham's story in Genesis 12:1–8 and 15:1–7.

Saint Paul talked about this greatness of God two thousand years ago. One day when he arrived in the ancient city of Athens, Greece, he looked around and saw that the city was filled with images of pagan gods. So he said to the people:

"You Athenians, I see that in every respect you are very religious. For as I walked around looking carefully at your shrines, I even discovered an altar inscribed, 'To an Unknown God.' What therefore you unknowingly worship, I proclaim to you. The God who made the world and all that is in it, the Lord of heaven and earth…is he who gives to everyone life and breath and everything" (Acts 17:22–25).

What was Paul saying to the people? In many ways he was praising the people for recognizing the footprints of God in creation. But he was also pointing out that they were worshiping an "Unknown God." They did not as yet know the God of Abraham, the God who had revealed himself as Lord of heaven and earth.

The words of Saint Paul remind us why the religions of Jews and Christians are different from all others. We believe in the one God, who revealed himself to us in a special way. It all began with Abraham. That is why both Jews and Christians are the descendants of Abraham. As we shall see, however, for Catholics and other Christians, God's revealing activity reached its high point in Jesus Christ.

And that is exactly what God did. God began the process by revealing himself to Abraham. What God did was something completely new for the human race, something unheard of by any other people. In Abraham, God was choosing a people for his own, inviting them into a close relationship with him. These people were the ancient Israelites, the ancestors of the Jews and our ancestors in faith, too. This revealing God would be their God, and they would be his people. God would not remain unknown to them; rather, he would be closer to them than they could ever imagine. So great would God be that no mere image or idol could contain him.

Because revelation is so basic to Catholic life, we should know its four most important features: (1) It happens over a long time. (2) It happens in history. (3) It happens between God and people. (4) It happens in community. Let's take a closer look at each of these features of revelation.

Over a Long Time   God chose to reveal himself gradually, over a long period, much as we ourselves do at times. As human beings we open ourselves to others as we get to know them better. We let others know about us little by little. It may even take a lifetime to get to know someone well.

If this is true for us, how much more so for God. That is because the mystery of God is so deep. It could never be revealed to us all at once; otherwise we would be overwhelmed by the majesty of God. The process of God revealing himself, therefore, has taken a long time. It began in a special way with Abraham and continued until it reached its high point in Jesus Christ. The New Testament explains God's revelation this way: "In times past, God spoke in partial and various ways to our ancestors through the prophets; in these last days, he spoke to us through a son" (Hebrews 1:1–2).

In History   God's revealing of himself did not just happen over time; it also happened in history. The exodus of the Israelites from slavery in Egypt, for example, was a real event. In that historical event the Israelites realized that God was with them and was responsible for freeing them from the hopelessness and despair of slavery. God was not just an impersonal bystander; he was personally involved in their lives. God continued to involve himself in the lives of the Israelites and their descendants. Then the greatest moment of God's involvement in human history happened: Jesus was born. In Jesus, God was not only involving himself in history; God became a part of our history.

Between God and People   God doesn't send us an encyclopedia or a CD-ROM to tell us about himself. God interacts with people; he has a relationship with them. That is how God reveals himself to people. Think of our ancestors in faith. God called Abraham, and Abraham and the people

Divine Revelation

How many times have you heard someone say that God loves you? How do you know it's true? How do we know that Jesus is really the Son of God? How do we know that God is even involved in our world and our lives?

We know the answers to these questions because God told us. The most important things we know about God come from one source: God himself. God making himself known to us is called *divine revelation*. It is called *divine* because it is an activity of God; it is called *revelation* because it is God making himself known to us in a deep and intimate way. Understanding divine revelation is essential to our whole life of faith. In fact it is the basis of everything Christians believe, and it helps to identify who we are as Catholics.

responded to God's call. God spoke to Moses at the burning bush. Moses and the people responded and entered into a covenant agreement with God. He would be their God; they would be his people. God spoke through the prophets and called the people to be true to the agreement they had made with God. Finally, God spoke to us in his Son and called us to discipleship.

We see, then, that revelation always happens between God and people. If we were to compare revelation with a conversation, it would not be a monologue, a one-sided conversation. It would be a dialogue with two sides: God on one side and us on the other.

In Community   God's revelation always takes place in a community setting. Even though God revealed himself to some individuals, such as Abraham and Moses, this revelation wasn't just for these individuals. God's revelation was for the whole community.

Is this community setting really important? It is very important! Human beings always depend on one another to get the "big picture" of things. Usually it takes the work of several people to clarify complicated issues. Think, for example,

how many people have contributed to our scientific understanding of the universe. No one person could have done the job. Think, too, of family and friends, of how often they help us to understand others and the events of our lives. So it is with our understanding of God's revelation. It would take the whole community to experience fully God's revealing activity, and it would take many individuals to understand and interpret it.

Are you surprised that revelation means so much? Are you surprised that God has been so active in our lives?

Catholic Teachings

About Revelation

The Church knows just how important revelation is and how important it is for us to understand it clearly. That is why all the bishops of the world talked about revelation at the Second Vatican Council. At this greatest of Church gatherings in our time, the bishops made sure everyone would know how important revelation is by writing an entire document about it.

From Generation to Generation

God not only revealed himself but made sure that his revelation would be passed on from generation to generation. How did this happen?

The Old Testament   In ancient Israel the story of God's revelation was handed on to the next generation by word of mouth. People talked, sang, and told their stories about the living experience of their community with God and all that God did for them. This handing on of their unwritten traditions by word of mouth is known as oral tradition. Later some of this oral tradition of the Israelites was written down under the guidance of the Holy Spirit. This written record of divine revelation came to be known as the Old Testament.

The Fullness of Revelation   Remember that God's revelation took place in the history of the community. It took place over a long period of time and reached its high point in Jesus Christ. That is why we say that what was recorded in the Old Testament was brought to completion in Christ our Lord. In him the fullness of God's revelation was made to us because God was speaking through his Son. For this reason Jesus was truly the Word of God. In Jesus, God spoke to us his fullest and final word. There will never be another. That is because Jesus brought the fullness of God's revelation to the world.

The New Testament   Filled with excitement about their experience of Jesus, the apostles and the first followers of Jesus wanted to share the good news. They wanted everyone to know what Jesus had taught them, why he came, and what he did for the world. This good news of Jesus was first handed on by the apostles and the early Church by word of mouth. Later some of this oral tradition was also put into writing under the guidance of the Holy Spirit. This written record of divine revelation came to be known as the New Testament.

The New Testament is the most important written record that comes to us from the time of the apostles and the early Church. Because it is a written document, it is permanent and cannot be changed. Neither can the Old Testament. Both are inspired by God. Catholics have a deep respect for both the Old and the New Testaments. Together they are known as Sacred Scripture.

 Name one way you can show reverence and respect for Sacred Scripture.

Is Scripture Alone Enough?

The answer to this question is no. Scripture can never stand alone. It needs tradition, the living experience of the community, to make it come alive. In fact, as we have seen, Scripture comes from the living tradition of the community. This living tradition existed before Scripture was written down and helped to form it.

Does Scripture give a complete picture of Jesus, the early Church, and all that God has revealed? No written record can do that. Even at the end of John's Gospel, for example, we read, "There are also many other things that Jesus did, but if these were to be described individually, I do not think the whole world would contain the books that would be written" (John 21:25). In a dramatic way John was telling us that no written record can completely capture a living experience.

Even though the New Testament may not give a complete picture of Jesus, it nevertheless gives a truthful and permanent picture. For example, the New Testament records the fact that Jesus died on the cross and rose from the dead. This truth cannot be denied or changed. The written word of Scripture gives us a constant guideline for our beliefs. The Church can never abandon, ignore, or change this written record.

It is also the responsibility of the Church to teach the true meaning of Scripture—that is, to interpret it—in every age. No type of written record can pass from generation to generation without being interpreted. That is why Scripture is truly a book of the Church.

It is clear, then, that the handing on of God's revelation comes to us through tradition and Scripture. These two are so closely related to each other that we cannot understand one without the other.

CATHOLIC ID

The handing on of revelation was described beautifully by Clement of Rome. He was a bishop of Rome and the earliest Christian writer outside the New Testament. Writing around A.D. 95, Clement said, "The apostles received the gospel for us from the Lord Jesus Christ; and Jesus Christ was sent forth from God. Christ, in other words, comes with a message from God, and the apostles with a message from Christ."

Saint Catherine of Siena (1347–1380)
The first woman to be named a
"Doctor of the Church"

A Great Treasure

The apostles and the early Church community realized that they had a great treasure to share with the whole world. And what was this treasure? The truths of revelation! Today Catholics call this treasure the deposit of faith. The *deposit of faith* includes all the truths entrusted, or handed over, by Christ to the apostles and the early Church. These truths, contained in tradition and Scripture, are now handed on by the Church as a treasure to the world.

Why do we call this treasure a *deposit*? The reason goes back to biblical times. Then a deposit was thought of as something special. It was so special, in fact, that a deposit was entrusted to someone to guard. That is why Saint Paul wrote to his companion Timothy and instructed him to hand on the whole message of revelation and to protect it from what was false. Paul wrote, "Guard what has been entrusted to you" (1 Timothy 6:20). Later he wrote to Timothy, "Guard this rich trust with the help of the holy Spirit…" (2 Timothy 1:14).

Paul must have thought that the deposit of faith was very important. That is why he used the words "rich trust" to describe it. The deposit of faith is important for us, too. It is that treasure entrusted to the Church by Christ until the end of time. It is a rich trust for us because it is about God's revelation, which lies at the very heart of our Catholic faith.

Scripture UPDATE

In the New Testament the short Letter of Jude, which is only twenty-five verses long, was written to warn the early Christians against false teachers. They were reminded that the teachings of the Church came from the preaching of the apostles, who were guided by the Holy Spirit. The community was to persevere in "the faith that was once for all handed down…" (Jude 3).

24

A Dynamic Treasure

As we have already said, the deposit of faith includes everything that God entrusted to the Church community in Scripture and tradition. Remember that Scripture means Old Testament and New Testament. Both were inspired by the Holy Spirit. But what is tradition? *Tradition* is the whole dynamic life and activity of the Church.

 Take a look at the chart to see what tradition includes and why it is so dynamic.

A Living Treasure

Being a deposit does not mean that the teachings of revelation are like a buried treasure or a museum piece to be preserved and dusted off from time to time. Rather the deposit of faith is a living thing, a dynamic treasure meant to be proclaimed and lived in each age. The Church guards this treasure by making it meaningful to all people throughout the world.

Will there be any further or new revelations from God to the community? No. The Church teaches that the fullness of God's revelation has come to us in Jesus Christ. God has told us in Jesus everything that we need to hear for every age. The community of the Church can never accept anything that would claim to go beyond Christ. Furthermore, any type of so-called private revelation—even if it is recognized by the Church—does not belong to the deposit of faith. Whatever God may have communicated since apostolic times to privileged individuals—for their own good or the good of the Church in a particular age—can add nothing to the deposit of faith.

The Church's Dynamic Life: Tradition's Many Parts		
Part	Description	Example
Teachings, customs, practices handed down from the time of the apostles	The handing on of the Church's dynamic life and beliefs either by word of mouth or in writing, but not necessarily found in Scripture	The practice of baptizing infants that has come down to us from the Church's earliest days
Creeds	Official statements of belief	Nicene Creed
Teachings of Church councils	Teachings from important gatherings of the world's bishops with the pope	Second Vatican Council (1962–1965)
Teachings from the Church Fathers	Writings from saintly scholars of the first eight centuries of the Church who helped to explain and hand on the Christian message	Clement of Rome, bishop of Rome around A.D. 95
The Church's worship and liturgy	The whole life and experience of the Church as it gathers together to worship God and hear God's word	God making himself known to us today as Scripture is proclaimed and preached at Mass

things to think about

What does it mean to you when we say that we are a people of tradition, that for Catholics the past is a living treasure and counts a great deal?

Sometimes we meet people who say that the answers to all life's questions can be found in the Bible. As a thoughtful Catholic would you agree or disagree with that statement? Why?

things to share

Imagine that you and a group of your friends were sent by Saint Paul to speak to the people of a great city like Athens. How would you prepare to speak to the people? What would you tell them about God's revelation to us?

Some people claim to have special messages from God, special "private" revelations. What should Catholics think about such things?

WORDS TO REMEMBER

Find and define the following:

divine revelation _____

_____

_____

deposit of faith _____

_____

_____

OnLine WITH THE PARISH

In the fourth century Saint Jerome complained to a friend about the sloppy way in which some Christians proclaimed the word of God. To read Scripture aloud without preparation was "circus stuff," he said. He meant that this was showing disrespect for God's word. Invite whoever trains lectors in your parish to talk with your group about this ministry. Explore the ways both lectors and listeners can treasure the word of God.

What do we mean when we say that God's revelation to us happens over a long period of time?

God ~~said~~ decided to revel himself slowley because that is how we revel ourselves to other people and there is too much to revel at once

Why is revelation at the very heart of our Catholic faith?

Why do we say that Scripture and tradition are so linked that one cannot stand without the other?

We say this Because Scripture was written of traditions and people and tradition takes after the scripture.

Name one part of tradition, explain it, and give an example.

One part of tradition is Creeds. Creeds are the official statments of belief. One creed is the Nicenecreed.

Why did Saint Paul say that the deposit of faith must be guarded as a "rich trust"?

In those day deposit meant something speceral so he called it rich trust. Faith must be gaurded like a deposit. That is why he wrote this.

Life in the Spirit

Saint Francis of Assisi was a master detective when it came to tracking God's footprints in creation. As a young seeker Francis spent hours hiking in the fields, admiring the beauty of flowers and the majesty of towering trees, climbing mountains, and walking in the rain. Each experience helped him to know God better. How can nature help you to open your heart to God?

DIVINE GIFT AND HUMAN RESPONSE

We walk by faith, not by sight.

2 Corinthians 5:7

ONE of the natural wonders of Yellowstone National Park in Wyoming is Old Faithful. This geyser shoots thousands of gallons of hot water and steam high into the air each time it spouts. Early explorers named it Old Faithful because it seemed to erupt "faithfully" every sixty-five or seventy minutes.

Further observation indicated that the eruptions of the geyser occur more irregularly than first thought. Nevertheless millions of tourists gather at the geyser each year, hoping to see the fountainlike column of water burst into the sky. They "believe" that Old Faithful will put on its spectacular performance once again for them.

What do the words "faithful," "believe," and "faith" mean to you? In terms of religion would you describe yourself as a faithful person? Are you a believer? What does faith mean to you?

Seeking the Truth

People express what is true or false for them in many ways. Some say, "I *think* that this is true, not that." Others say, "I *believe* that this is true, not that." Still others might say, "I *know* that this is true, not that." Do all these expressions mean the same thing? Or does our choice of words make a difference?

If we say that we *think* something is true, we are expressing our opinion about something. For example, a farmer may say, "I think that I will have a very big harvest this year. My crops will grow well because of abundant rainfall, no floods, and plenty of good weather." The farmer is expressing an opinion about the future and is fairly certain that this thought will come true.

If we say that we *know* something is true, it means that we are absolutely certain that something will happen. We base our knowledge on concrete facts. For example, scientists have developed vaccines against terrible diseases such as polio, measles, and mumps. Over many years of experimentation and testing, they had visible proof and knew that the vaccines would work to save many lives. We know that the vaccines work today.

If we say that we *believe* in or *have faith* in something or someone, we are putting our trust in our past experiences or in someone else. Belief is generally the result of putting our trust in another person. For example, you hear a rumor that your best friend has been caught shoplifting. He or she tells you that this is a lie. You believe your friend because in the past he or she has always been truthful and reliable. You trust your friend and believe in his or her innocence.

It may sound strange to some people, but much of what we know comes through faith. Think about this: Have you ever been to Antarctica? Most of us have not, but we believe that Antarctica exists. Others have been there and have told us about it. We have seen pictures and videos. We can point to it on a map. It is reasonable to accept the fact that Antarctica exists. It would be unreasonable for us to deny its reality and to say that Antarctica was dreamed up on a Hollywood set or designed from a computer model. People would think that we were crazy. So although we have never been to Antarctica ourselves, we believe, on the basis of the experience of others, that it does exist.

In many ways, then, to live is to believe. To be a person of belief does not mean that we live in a fantasy world or a world filled with doubts. Our beliefs are certain because they are reasonable. Nevertheless belief, or faith, includes a risk. We may, for example, put our trust in the wrong person or make a wrong judgment about our experience. But we take these risks every day. We place our trust in people day in and day out. We accept the existence of things that we cannot see or touch ourselves.

How can we possibly continue to live if we do not have faith? Think of the many simple ways in which you live by faith each day. Which one means the most to you? Why?

31

Religious Faith

Each day when we awaken, we share an unspoken faith that the sun will rise and set, that the pull of gravity will keep us firmly planted on earth, and that the atmosphere will be good enough for us to breathe. We also have faith in people, especially members of our family, our friends, and those in whom we place our trust. We call this type of faith natural faith, since it has to do with our everyday experience of the natural world.

There is, however, another type of faith. This kind of faith is religious faith. It is the basis for our personal relationship with God. Religious faith is not only faith in something; it is faith in Someone. It is faith in God.

To understand this kind of faith, we can turn to Abraham. In the Old Testament he is presented as the model of faith. Remember the story of Abraham told in Genesis 12—22. God promised to make him the father of many nations despite the fact that Abraham and Sarah, his wife, were both beyond the normal age for becoming parents. Later Abraham was called to offer his only son, Isaac, as a sacrifice to God. Even though Abraham's heart was broken at the thought of losing Isaac, Abraham's faith never wavered. He was ready to risk everything for God.

God rewarded Abraham's faith by sparing Isaac's life. The faith of Abraham had been tested by God. God showed that he was true to the agreement he had made with Abraham: All the nations of the earth would share in God's blessing through Isaac because of Abraham's faith.

In the Bible the word *faith* means "to hold firm to." Faith in God is a holding on to God; we anchor our lives on his word. We can do this because God alone is worthy of our complete trust. God alone is our strength. Jesus reminded us of this when he said that all things are possible for those who believe. Faith is so important that even a small amount of faith can "move" mountains (Matthew cf. 17:20).

 Describe a time when you felt that you could move mountains.

A Gift from God

How do we get faith? Do we arrive at faith on our own? To answer these questions, we must get to the heart of what faith really is. And that is God's grace.

Grace is a gift from God and a participation in the very life of God. The grace of faith enables us to begin to know God as God knows himself. That is why faith is a virtue; it is a power. Faith gives us the power to go beyond our human understanding and beyond what we can see and feel and touch around us. We cannot do this on our own. Faith empowers us to see through the "eyes of God." This means that faith is a supernatural gift from God; it is a gift that goes beyond our natural powers. As Saint Paul says, "We walk by faith, not by sight" (2 Corinthians 5:7).

Does this mean that without God's grace we cannot have faith? Are we incapable on our own of believing all that God has revealed? Yes, that is exactly what we are saying! God's grace and our free cooperation with it are essential to faith.

Without grace our human powers alone cannot enable us to be people of faith. The reason for this is that by faith we know God and God's revelation through the knowledge God has of himself. This sort of knowledge obviously goes beyond our natural powers. This is why Saint Paul could say, "For by grace you have been saved through faith, and this is not from you; it is the gift of God" (Ephesians 2:8).

We can say, then, that *faith* is a supernatural gift from God. It enables us to open ourselves to God and to accept all that God has revealed. When we have faith, we know God through the knowledge God has of himself. In this sense faith is actually the beginning of eternal life, in which we shall know God "face to face."

Describing Faith

Faith comes from "what is heard." It is not like the study of history, which comes from digging up facts and researching past events. Faith depends, not on our brilliance or position in the world, but on what we hear and on what we accept. In Scripture we read:

> For "everyone who calls on the name of the Lord will be saved." But how can they call on him in whom they have not believed? And how can they believe in him of whom they have not heard? And how can they hear without someone to preach? And how can people preach unless they are sent?...Thus faith comes from what is heard, and what is heard comes through the word of Christ.
> Romans 10:13–17

Does this mean that faith is blind, that we accept anything, even if it is totally unreasonable? In no way! Faith has some definite characteristics, or qualities.

Reasonable   The first quality of faith is that it is reasonable; it is not blind. God has made human beings intelligent creatures. God wants us to understand as much as we can about our faith; this means that we have to ask questions. Faith always seeks understanding.

The power of human reason, our ability to think things out, should never be in conflict with faith. That is because God is the source of both faith and reason. The more we use our reason and intelligence to investigate the world, the more we see God's creative hand at work. God cannot contradict the truth of what he has created. For example, God cannot make a square circle because the nature of a square and that of a circle are directly opposed to each other.

Faith does not take the place of reason, personal experience, human searching, or learning from others. Faith builds on our human abilities and works through them.

 What are some of the questions you have in seeking to understand your faith?

Certain   The second quality of faith is that it is certain. This is because faith rests on God's word and God cannot lie. As we read in Scripture, "If we accept human testimony, the testimony of God is surely greater" (1 John 5:9).

Does this mean that all the truths of our faith will be perfectly clear to us or that we will somehow remove the mystery of faith? No. It simply means that we may not grasp or understand everything right away or completely.

The funny thing about human beings is that we would like everything to be simple, without any complications. But real life is not like that; it is complex. If we look in a mathematics book, for example, we are going to find that some ideas are difficult to grasp at first. But we shouldn't be afraid of the challenge of new ideas. The same can be said of science, technology, history, or geography. Why should people expect anything different when it comes to the truths of faith? We do not have to be geniuses to accept our faith, but we do have to work hard to understand it according to our abilities. Faith is more than just a feeling.

Free   The fourth quality of faith is that it is free. When we place our faith and trust in God, we do so freely; God does not force us to believe against our will. If this were not so, faith would be against our human dignity as created by God.

Professed   The fifth quality of faith is that it must be professed. By this we mean that faith is not just held inside us; it must also be expressed by our actions and by our words. This means that we must give witness to our faith. It is not just something that we think about. Faith that is not lived and professed is, in fact, unbelief.

 *What do you find most challenging in living and giving witness to your faith?*

Communal   The third quality of faith is that it is communal. When we respond in faith to God's revelation, we do so as individuals, but not in isolation from others. Faith happens in a community. This is the way God deals with humankind—through a community. We receive faith through the Church, just as we receive life through our parents. We did not give ourselves faith, just as we did not give ourselves life. Faith, therefore, is not simply a personal, solitary act.

CATHOLIC ID   You may notice that Catholics use the word *faith* in two different ways. We might say, "That person is a person of faith." This use of the word refers to faith as a virtue, as the grace of faith. We might also say, "I live by my Catholic faith." This use of the word refers to what we believe, or the content of faith.

35

A Lifelong Challenge

Some people feel that their religious education, the exploration of their faith, ends in the eighth grade or after celebrating the sacraments of initiation: Baptism, Confirmation, and Eucharist. They feel that after these celebrations there is nothing left to learn. But such an idea could not be further from the truth. Exploring our faith is a lifetime project.

Our faith is a priceless gift, but it can lose its luster or even be lost altogether. How can we make sure this does not happen? We do this first of all by taking the time to learn about our faith. This involves more than just memorizing facts or names or dates. It means exploring our faith so deeply that it will make a real difference in our lives. After all, how can we really appreciate something unless we know more about it?

Besides learning about our faith, we must also nourish it by the way we live our lives. We do this through the life-giving relationship we have with God in prayer. At the center of our prayer life are the Eucharist and the other sacraments. We also grow in faith when we actively participate in the life of the Church. Faith never stands alone but is lived by a community of people.

What happens if we do not explore our faith, or nourish it in prayer, or participate in the faith life of the community? Our faith will grow weak. Then, one day, there may be nothing left of it to hold on to. We would have wasted God's precious gift to us. But this will not happen if we take up the lifelong challenge of growing in faith.

Living Without Faith

Generally speaking there are two kinds of people who seem to live their lives without faith. They are called atheists and agnostics.

Atheists *Atheists* are people who deny the existence of God and who, therefore, live their lives without God. Although we may not know any individuals who claim to be atheists, many people seem to live as if they were atheists. This includes people who never think about God. It also includes people who speak highly about faith and religion but leave it at that level, the level of talking. Actions speak louder than words, however. Catholics who loudly proclaim that they are members of the Church but never practice their faith are, in fact, living an atheistic lifestyle.

Are atheists by definition bad people? Of course not! Some people practice no formal religion and are convinced that God does not exist. But many of them care very deeply about living a life full of values, including care for others, care for the earth, and striving for peace.

Why, then, are they atheists? There are many possible reasons. One may be that no one has ever approached them to bring them the good news of the gospel. Another reason may be that these nonbelievers spoke with believers who did not seem to have intelligent explanations about what they believe. Perhaps the nonbelievers met people who claimed to be religious but gave poor example, turning them off to God. Another reason may be that they rejected the gift of faith that God offered to them. Whatever the reason, we can never judge others, since we do not know their circumstances.

Agnostics *Agnostics* are people who cannot decide whether or not to believe in God. They say that God's existence or the answers to life's most important questions are unknowable at best and are even unprovable. They seem to put their trust only in those things that can be seen or felt or heard or touched or experienced in a physical way.

Knowing how wonderful faith is, we can say that people without faith do not know what they are missing. That is because faith is participation in the very life of God and the knowledge God has of himself. Does this mean that we as people of faith can never have moments of doubt in our lives? No. We would not be human if we did not have some doubts. But as believers we can always turn to Jesus. Remember, it was Jesus who said, "Do not let your hearts be troubled. You have faith in God; have faith also in me" (John 14:1).

 What advice would you give to someone who seems to be having problems with faith?

Scripture UPDATE

There are many places in the gospels in which Jesus speaks about faith. One time he was talking about the gift of faith and said, "No one can come to me unless the Father who sent me draw him" (John 6:44). Another time Jesus was talking about faith to the apostle Thomas, who had doubted Jesus' resurrection and would only be satisfied with visible proof. Jesus said, "Blessed are those who have not seen and have believed" (John 20:29). What do these words of Jesus say to you?

things to think about

Call to mind your favorite TV programs, movies, and songs. In what ways do they explore or encourage religious faith?

Should we consider people who do not believe in God to be bad people? Why or why not?

How would you respond to the following statement: No one can tell me what to believe. Faith is only a personal matter.

WORDS TO REMEMBER

Find and define the following:

faith _____
_____
_____

atheists _____
_____
_____

things to share

People who do not have faith do not know what they are missing. What do you as a person of faith think that they are missing?

Suppose you met someone who said to you, "People of faith never have any doubts." How would you respond to that person?

OnLine
WITH THE PARISH

God has called us to be members of a faith community. Alone we are like twigs, easily broken. Together we are like redwoods, whose strength and beauty inspire confidence and awe. Young people especially need to experience themselves as vital members of the parish community. Consider the ways in which your group can help young people to feel more at home in the parish. Plan a project to reach out to those who seem to be outside of parish life.

Is it possible to have faith without God's grace? Explain.

No because faith is a gift from God.

1

What is the difference between knowing and believing?

If you know something then you are positive it is real and have seen it, if you believe something you just think it is real but have never seen it.

2

Explain what we mean when we say that faith is a supernatural gift from God.

It is a gift because if it wasn't for faith we wouldn't have any proof God existed.

3

Why must faith be reasonable?

Because if it ~~wasn't~~ isn't reasonable then how could anyone belive it.

4

What do you think it would be like to live without faith?

It would be a lot different. You would have nothing to look forward to when you die and nothing to berive in to help you along.

5

Life
in the Spirit

A great Catholic writer named Thomas Merton once described faith as "the opening of an inward eye, the eye of the heart." Into that open "eye" flows the light of God's truth. And in that truth we find the meaning of our existence. Go to a quiet place where you can be in communion (union) with God. Close your eyes and ask the Holy Spirit to open the eye of your heart. Pray inwardly, "Let the light of your truth flow into me." Be still.

THE GOD WHO REVEALS

CHAPTER 4

Glory to God in the highest.

Luke 2:14

HOW do we know that God exists?
Can we prove God's existence?

Arguing for God

Ever since people began to think about the origin of the world and the meaning of life, they have wondered whether or not God exists.

The greatest thinkers of humanity have struggled with this question. Some of them have tried to prove that God exists. Of course they were not thinking of proof in the scientific sense of the word. God and the life of faith cannot be analyzed in a test tube. God's existence cannot be proved in a laboratory.

What these great thinkers did come up with were a number of convincing arguments for the existence of God. These arguments point to God and offer a reasonable basis for faith. We will look at three of the arguments.

The First Cause One argument for the existence of God can be called the "nothing is caused by itself" argument. It begins with the idea that everything must have a cause, an explanation for its origin. When we see a beautifully carved statue, for example, the first question we ask is, "Who was the artist?" We know that such a fine work of art was not simply found in a quarry as a finished piece. It took time and talent for a sculptor to carve it and make it a work of art.

The same can be said of the universe. We look around and ask, "Where did this marvel come from? What caused the universe and our solar system?" An immediate answer might be that it evolved to its present state over billions of years.

But then the next question must be, "What caused evolution in the first place?" We can continue with a thousand questions and answers, but at the end the same question can be asked: "What caused that?" When we finally arrive at a first cause, we reach the end of the line. Beyond this First Cause we can go no further. And that First Cause is God! Nobody caused God to be. Nobody made God.

42

What can be said about a computer or an eye also applies to the universe. It, too, is a complex and magnificent masterpiece. The argument from design suggests that the universe did not happen by chance but had an intelligent designer. This Great Designer is God.

The Unmoved Mover   Another famous argument for the existence of God is based on movement and change. It is called the "unmoved mover" argument. From your study of science, you know that all things are in motion. Look at an atom, for example, and you will see moving electrons. The whole universe, in fact, is in motion and is evolving. Movement, of course, begins when something is moved by something else. But where did all this movement start? When we go back as far as we can go, we arrive at the point of a first mover. This Unmoved Mover is God.

These are some of the arguments for God's existence that have been proposed by the greatest thinkers of humanity. They are not proofs in the scientific sense, but they do make us think. They are reasonable ways to God; they are argued invitations to faith.

The Great Designer   The next argument can be called the "argument from design." Think of the computer on your desk or in the library. It did not assemble itself from bits of metal and plastic. It is the product of intelligent design and skilled construction. Or consider the marvel of human sight and the complexity of the human eye. When you look at an object, reflected light from the object enters the eye through the pupil. The optic nerve immediately carries the image of the object to the brain, which interprets what you are seeing. What a masterpiece the eye is! Do you think this wonderful organ came about by chance? Or was there an intelligent cause behind it?

 If you were going to give an argument for God's existence, what would it be?

God and Reason

Reason, the power we have to figure things out, can go a long way in helping us to understand who God is. When we look at the world around us, we see beauty, harmony, and order. Reasonable people say that someone must have designed the world with these things in mind.

What do we find in Scripture about God and reason? In Wisdom 13:1–9 we read that people can come to the knowledge of the one true God through the beauty and goodness seen in creation. After all, it makes sense to say that the author of the universe must be far superior and more wonderful than the world we see.

Saint Paul made this point in his New Testament letter to the Romans. Paul was very clear. He scolded those who refused to be reasonable and who turned to the worship of idols instead of God. Paul said:

> For what can be known about God is evident to them, because God made it evident to them. Ever since the creation of the world, his invisible attributes of eternal power and divinity have been able to be understood and perceived in what he has made. As a result, they have no excuse; for although they knew God they did not accord him glory as God or give him thanks.
> Romans 1:19–21

Perhaps Saint Paul was reminded of the famous line, "Fools say in their hearts, 'There is no God'" (Psalm 14:1).

Can human reason provide all the answers we need? No. Reason can take us only so far in our search for God. It cannot tell us much beyond the fact that a personal and caring God fashioned the world. For everything else we depend upon God to tell us about himself. We already know this from our study of revelation and faith. Divine revelation is the basis of our knowledge about God and our faith in God.

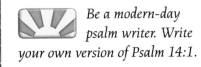

Be a modern-day psalm writer. Write your own version of Psalm 14:1.

God and Revelation

One truth that is basic to our Jewish-Christian heritage is that God is a personal God. God can never be reduced to being just a force of nature or a nameless power in the universe. Nor is God a lifeless image or idol to be worshiped. Our God is alive, and from the Old Testament we even learn God's name.

In ancient times the name of a person or thing was far more important than it is for us today. For the biblical writers, to know someone's name was to know that person. To have no name was to have no existence at all. In fact, to give a name was a powerful act. It was to give someone or something an identity. That is one reason God is described in Genesis as naming everything he created.

Now we can see why it was important to know God's name in Old Testament times. By revealing his name, God was identifying himself to us. Do you remember the story of Moses at the burning bush? It was from there that God sent Moses to the people. When Moses asked what he should tell his people about the God of their ancestors, God revealed to Moses the divine name. God said that his name was *Yahweh*, which means "I am who am" (Exodus 3:14).

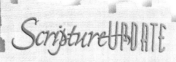

Scripture UPDATE

Have you ever pictured God whistling? The biblical writers did. They described God in wonderfully human terms. In the *New American Bible* translation, we read in Zechariah 10:8 that God whistles to gather his people together.

God had a name! Yahweh was like no other name. Moses was to say to God's people, "I AM sent me to you" (Exodus 3:14). God's name showed the people that he was like no other god that could be imagined. Yahweh was the God who would personally save the people from slavery and make with them an everlasting covenant.

What else do we find out about God in the Old Testament? Yahweh is described as the living God. The writers of the Old Testament wanted it perfectly understood that God was not a lifeless idol of wood or stone but truly a living being. They even described God in human terms. In their descriptions Yahweh has a face with eyes, ears, mouth, and nostrils. He has hands and feet. He speaks, hears, smells, laughs, whistles, and walks. He feels joy, anger, hatred, love, disgust, and compassion. We know, of course, that God is not a human being with hands and feet. The biblical writers used these images to make their message clear: The living God communicates to his people and is thoroughly involved in their lives.

God the Creator

God is the creator of all things. God created by his word; he spoke and everything came into being. That is the truth of faith we learn from the first page of the Bible. Creation is the creator's first word to us.

For many centuries people believed that all the statements in the Bible should be taken literally—exactly, word for word. That is why they thought that the universe was created literally in seven days as described in Genesis and that this took place about four thousand years before Christ. Some people still believe this.

In contrast modern science estimates that our universe is billions of years old. Scientists have different ideas of explaining how the universe began and how it evolved. Some think that a "big bang," or cosmic explosion of matter, eventually produced the whole universe. What should Catholics think? Should we be afraid of science?

Interpreting the Creation Story

The inspired writers of Genesis were not interested in giving a scientific treatment of creation. Rather they wanted to tell the truths of faith. They also wanted to make clear the difference between their beliefs and those of their Mesopotamian neighbors, who followed pagan religions with many gods.

To understand the message of Genesis correctly, we must understand what the inspired authors had in mind when they were writing this book. Far from a scientific approach, these writers used the language of poetry to get their message across, telling the truth in "symbolic" and "figurative" language (*Catechism*, 362, 390). They wanted to point to truths that were unique to their understanding of God, that were not shared by other peoples.

In the Mesopotamian creation accounts, pagan gods had beginnings like mortal human beings. The biblical writers rejected this idea. They stressed that in the beginning God created the heavens and earth and everything in them. By doing so they were teaching that in the beginning there was nothing but God; then God created. God always was. He had no beginning.

The Genesis writers taught that there was only one God, the creator of everything. Unlike the pagan gods, the God of Israel existed before everything else. He was the *creator*: He created everything from nothing. God spoke, and by his word all things came into being.

How could the biblical writers best share their ideas with others? They told a story that pictured God as a worker who labored for six days of the week and rested on the seventh day—just as the people of Israel did. Thus, the biblical authors imagined God doing what a human worker might do. The first thing needed in a workshop would be light. So on the first day God created light. It did not matter to the writers that in their story the sun, moon, and stars would not be created until the fourth day.

The real message of Genesis, then, is about faith. It was never meant to deal with modern, scientific questions, but it is not opposed to science either. The Genesis account tells us *that* God created, not *how* God created. This is essential for Catholics to know and understand.

Faith and Science

Using telescopes, scientists peer into the vast reaches of space, hoping to unravel the mystery of the universe. Such scientific investigations have led to many theories. Through them we have come to see that the universe and all life evolved over billions of years. The inspired writers of Genesis, however, were not familiar with the theory of evolution. They were interested in teaching only one idea: Everything was made by God. This was the truth they wanted to share.

Today we know that science and religion are different. But they are not enemies; they both seek the truth. The Church welcomes the findings of science. To know more about the scientific details of creation is to know more about God the creator. However, such scientific knowledge will never replace the truth of Genesis—that God created the whole universe.

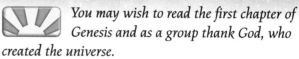 *You may wish to read the first chapter of Genesis and as a group thank God, who created the universe.*

CATHOLIC TEACHINGS

About God the Creator

The Church teaches us that God did not create the world and then leave it alone. God's work did not end with the act of creation. The whole universe continues to exist because God keeps it in existence. God's work of creation continues.

Attributes of God

Besides the word *creator*, there are other words that we use to describe God alone. These are God's attributes, or characteristics. The attributes of God, the supreme Being, include eternal, almighty, all-knowing, and all-present.

Eternal   Think about the time it would take to travel to galaxies that are millions of light-years away from us. For God these millions of years would be like an "instant." This is because God is eternal: He always was and always will be.

It may be hard for us to understand, but God is not subject to time as we are. Time is a measurable period that has a before and an after. But God is without beginning or end. God lives in eternity and has no need for time. Time is part of creation, but God is not part of creation. God is above it; God is timeless.

Material things change and pass away; God remains and is changeless. Creatures are subject to change because they are subject to time. Therefore they are finite; they have an end. God is infinite; he has no end. He is not limited by time.

Almighty   When we say that God is almighty, we mean that God can do all things. Another word for almighty is *omnipotent*. Who but the almighty God could create the universe and keep it in existence?

When we say that God is almighty, do we mean that he can do anything, even the impossible? Not at all. Just as God cannot make a square circle, since this would be a contradiction, it is impossible for God to commit a sin. That would make God imperfect and exactly like his creatures. God is perfect and could never do anything that goes against his perfection.

Can the almighty God work miracles? The answer is yes. Miracles are wonderful events that cannot be fully explained by the laws of nature. Miracles are done only by God for a purpose and show forth God's care and power.

The Church does not discourage people from praying for miracles, but it remains cautious about miracles in general. Whenever someone claims that a miracle has taken place, the Church first looks for a natural cause to explain it. Then, after a thorough investigation, only the Church declares whether or not a true miracle has occurred.

All-Knowing   Because God is eternal, he knows everything past, present, and future. Another word for all-knowing is *omniscient*. Does the fact that God is all-knowing mean that human beings are like puppets on a string? that we have no freedom? The answer is no.

An example may give us a rough idea of the way the all-knowing God interacts with us. Suppose you are standing on top of the World Trade Center in New York City, 110 stories above the ground. As you look down, you see two cars turning a corner from opposite directions and about ready to collide. You know that they will crash into each other. But the knowledge of this event, which you have before it happens, does not control the crash. So it is with God. God's knowledge of events does not control our choices or destroy our freedom to live a full human life.

All-Present God is everywhere. Another word for this attribute of God is *omnipresent*. To say that God is all-present does not mean that we need to make room for him on the seat next to us—as if we were talking about God as occupying space the way we do. God is present by the fact that he created everything and keeps everything in existence. Just as God is not limited by time, so God is not limited as we are by space. That is because God is a spirit. This means that God is not a material being; God is not made of matter and has no material parts.

Have you ever noticed at Mass how often God's attributes are mentioned? Look through the prayers of the liturgy and see how many of them you can find.

CATHOLIC ID
Are you interested in taking care of God's creation? If so, you may wish to take Saint Francis of Assisi as your patron. He is the patron saint of all ecologists. Saint Francis reminded us that the created world is God's work of art. The all-powerful God filled it with value and beauty. As Catholics we should take the lead in caring for God's creation and never neglect it.

things to think about

An author wrote that people's idea of God was too small. After reading this chapter, has your idea of God expanded or contracted?

Why do you think some people get upset when they learn from science that the world was not created by God in six or seven days? How would you explain the Catholic position on the creation of the world?

WORDS TO REMEMBER

Find and define the following:

Yahweh _____
_____
_____

creator _____
_____
_____

things to share

Suppose that you tell your best friend that you want to be a scientist. Your friend says that no one can be a good Catholic and a good scientist at the same time. Share your responses to your friend with the group.

Your topic for an upcoming speech to young people is "Get with It: Believe in God!" Outline your talk, highlighting the main points.

OnLine WITH THE PARISH

As a sign of respect for God's creation and for God our creator, get permission to sponsor an environmental day. Your group may want to take the lead in organizing something as simple as a clean-up day on the parish grounds.

How do we know that God exists? Can we prove God's existence? Why or why not?

1

Can reason alone provide answers to all our questions about God?

2

In the Genesis creation accounts, how is the one true God described differently from the gods of the pagans?

3

What do we mean when we say that God is eternal?

4

What do we mean when we say that God is all-knowing?

5

Life in the Spirit

Many of the saints spent a great deal of time coming to understand the meaning of Psalm 14:1, which says, "Fools say in their hearts, 'There is no God.'" Most people do wonder about God's existence at one time or another. The important thing, though, is that this questioning can be a time of growth and change—if we are willing to do the hard work and take time to understand who God is. Are you willing to do this?

THE GOD WHO IS

Worthy are you, LORD our God,
to receive glory and honor and power.

Revelation 4:11

53

HAVE you ever tried to picture God? Great artists such as Michelangelo pictured God as an older man with white hair and a beard. Does that sound like your picture of God, or is yours different?

Unlike Any Other

Our Old Testament ancestors in faith were forbidden to make any image of God. The reason for this is that God is a spirit. God also surpasses and goes beyond anything he has made. This surpassing excellence of God is called God's *transcendence*.

The ancient pagan gods were thought of as little more than superhuman beings. The biblical writers could never accept such a limited idea of the one true God. When they wrote of God, they wanted to stress the fact that God is totally different from us and the world around us. Think of the experience Moses had at the burning bush. When he began to approach the bush, God said, "Come no nearer! Remove the sandals from your feet" (Exodus 3:5). Moses stood trembling before the majesty of God. He knew that God was absolutely unlike any other being.

The most important word the biblical writers used to describe God's transcendence was the word *holy*. One of the most dramatic scenes in the Old Testament is based on the holiness of God. One day the prophet Isaiah went into the Temple of Jerusalem. There he had what he described as an overwhelming experience of God:

> I saw the Lord seated on a high and lofty throne, with the train of his garment filling the temple. Seraphim were stationed above; each of them had six wings: with two they veiled their faces, with two they veiled their feet, and with two they hovered aloft. "Holy, holy, holy is the LORD of hosts!" they cried one to the other. "All the earth is filled with his glory!" At the sound of that cry, the frame of the door shook and the house was filled with smoke.
> Isaiah 6:1–4

In magnificent images Isaiah attempts to share with us his experience of the transcendent God. God is pictured in great majesty, sitting on a throne. He is being worshiped and adored by the seraphim, six-winged creatures that often appeared in ancient Near Eastern art. In later times this heavenly court of God was identified with the angels. Using two of their wings, the seraphim covered their faces because no creature would dare to look upon God. Using two more wings, they covered their feet to keep a respectful distance from God. Finally, with the last two wings, they held themselves aloft as a way of showing God adoration and worship.

In Isaiah's scene the seraphim sing of God's holiness. They repeat the word *holy* three times to show that God is all holy, that God's holiness is endless. Only God is worthy of praise and complete adoration. God's *holiness* is another word for his otherness, his transcendence. God is completely apart from anything that he created. Isaiah highlighted this by concluding his vision of God's majesty with smoke filling the Temple. Smoke was a symbol for the presence of the transcendent God.

What are we to make of this scene from Isaiah? To say that God is holy means much more than the fact that God is good. Holiness is the essential characteristic of God. It tells us of his perfection, otherness, and total transcendence. God is completely apart from anything created; God is not one of his creatures.

God alone is holy. This statement may be surprising to those of us who think that we can be holy, too. But the source of all holiness is God. If we are holy, it is because we have been given a share in God's perfection. Our holiness is never our own; God alone is holy. Only he is worthy of our adoration and praise.

As we shall see, we have been called into a very intimate relationship with God. God is close to us. But we can never forget that God is transcendent. Otherwise we run the risk of thinking about God as only a creature like ourselves. Then to whom would we sing "holy, holy, holy"?

 Have you ever had an experience of God's transcendence? Recall it.

Tell about those things that help you remember God's awesome transcendence, such as the vastness of space and a beautiful sunset.

The Old Testament celebrated God's transcendence in many ways. One way biblical writers expressed it was by writing about angels. In biblical times, God often revealed himself and acted indirectly through angels. The very word *angel*, which means "messenger," tells us what these creatures of God do. Recall the story of the angel Raphael, who brought God's message of hope to a suffering family. He also offered the prayers of God's people in the presence of the transcendent God (Tobit 12:12–15).

In the Old Testament we also find another way of expressing God's transcendence. This was done by substituting other words for the sacred name, Yahweh. This name was so holy that it was hardly ever spoken. The writers used terms such as the "face" of the Lord (Exodus 33:23), the "name" of the Lord (Exodus 20:24), and the "glory" of the Lord (1 Kings 8:11). This same devotion to God's name carried over into the New Testament. Matthew, for example, referred to the kingdom of heaven rather than the kingdom of God.

The Lord's Prayer sums up many Old Testament ideas about God's transcendence. It is significant that this prayer begins with the petition "hallowed be thy name." Here we are repeating the Old Testament practice of referring to God's name rather than referring directly to God.

In the opening address to God, we say "who art in heaven," suggesting that God is totally different from us. But at the same time we say "Our Father," reminding us of God's closeness to us. He who is in "heaven" and who is yet "Our Father" brings out the wonderful contrast between God's transcendence and God's nearness in our Christian experience.

Celebrating God's Grandeur

For thousands of years Catholics have used architecture and music to express their belief in the transcendence of God. Think of magnificent cathedrals soaring hundreds of feet into the air, built to praise God. The grandeur of architecture, stained glass, and music lifts our spirits to God.

Like the people of the Old Testament, we also think of God when we see the rising smoke and smell the fragrant fumes of incense, which we sometimes use at liturgy. As the psalmist says, "Let my prayer be incense before you; my uplifted hands an evening sacrifice" (Psalm 141:2).

Celebrating God's Closeness

Just as we speak of God's otherness by using the word *transcendence*, so we use another word when speaking of God's closeness to us. That word is *immanence*. We know that God is immanent, or close to us: "For what great nation is there that has gods so close to it as the LORD, our God, is to us whenever we call upon him?" (Deuteronomy 4:7).

The prophets constantly reminded the people of God's closeness. They did this by using very human images to show the closeness of God to his people. The prophet Hosea, for example, imagined God showing the love and tenderness of a parent, guiding his children in taking their first steps, lifting them in his arms, and healing their injuries (Hosea 11:3–4).

This nearness of God reaches its highest point in Jesus. God is so close to us in Jesus that Saint Paul writes, "You received a spirit of adoption, through which we cry, '*Abba*, Father!'. . . We are children of God, and if children, then heirs, heirs of God and joint heirs with Christ…" (Romans 8:15–17). How much more immanent, or close, can God be to us, his adopted children?

CATHOLIC TEACHINGS

About Angels

God created all things "seen and unseen." Catholics believe that angels are a part of this unseen creation. The Church teaches that all during life we are surrounded by the watchful care and intercession of the angels.

Angels are created spirits. This means they do not have material parts. They are also intelligent beings. Nevertheless they are still creatures, just as human beings are creatures. These messengers of God, who are mentioned again and again in the Old Testament, are spoken of frequently in the New Testament as well. For example, a multitude of angels, "the heavenly host," sang God's praises at the birth of Jesus (Luke 2:8–14). The Church celebrates two special feasts in honor of the angels: on September 29 (the Archangels Michael, Gabriel, and Raphael) and October 2 (the Guardian Angels).

The Triune God

What is the transcendent God really like?

After God gradually revealed himself over many centuries, humanity was finally given the most marvelous insight of all: God's people were introduced to the mystery of the Blessed Trinity. This is the central belief of Christian faith and life. By the *Blessed Trinity* we mean that there are three Persons in one God. The one and only God is Father, Son, and Holy Spirit.

What do we mean when we say that there are three Persons in one God? Are *Father*, *Son*, and *Holy Spirit* just different names for one and the same Being? Not at all! The Church teaches that the three Persons in the one God are distinct from one another and equal to one another. God is triune: three and one at the same time. God is not one with three parts; God is completely one and completely three.

We believe that the three Persons in one God are distinct from one another:
- The Father is not the Son or the Holy Spirit.
- The Son is not the Father or the Holy Spirit.
- The Holy Spirit is not the Father or the Son.

We also believe that these three Persons, who are distinct from one another, are equally God:
- The Father is God.
- The Son is God.
- The Holy Spirit is God.

 You may wish to use the accompanying chart to help you remember these ideas.

Thinking about the Blessed Trinity

THE FATHER — IS — GOD

IS NOT

IS NOT

THE SON

IS NOT

THE HOLY SPIRIT — IS

A Clear Understanding

It took a long time for Christians to work out these details about the Trinity. In their search for an understanding, the first Christians did not have a library of religion books from which they could get answers to their questions. An understanding of the Blessed Trinity had to be developed, and this took time.

During the third century a priest by the name of Arius made one of the first efforts to give a clear explanation of the Trinity. He tried his best but made a fundamental mistake and was in error. Arius taught that God could not create the material world directly because God is transcendent. He would have to do this through someone else. That someone else was the Son. This meant, of course, that for Arius the Son was created and not transcendent; therefore the Son was not God. Look again at the chart to see why Arius was so wrong.

What was the reaction of the Church community? Arius' mistaken ideas began to spread, and a great controversy developed in the Church. People grew alarmed; even Emperor Constantine was concerned for the peace of his empire. That is why the bishops of the Church, who are responsible for correct doctrine, gathered in the city of Nicaea (in present-day Turkey) in A.D. 325.

It took the bishops a long time to work out and agree on the precise terms that would correctly define the doctrine of the Trinity for Catholics.

Icon of the Blessed Trinity, Andrei Rublev, circa 1410

To make it clear that the Son is God, just as the Father is God, the bishops said that the Son was "one in Being" with the Father. The teachings that emerged from the Council of Nicaea are the basis of the Nicene Creed, which we profess today at Mass. We, too, proclaim that the Son is "one in Being with the Father."

Why is it so important for us to know and understand all this? Does it have anything to do with our lives? It has everything to do with our lives! We have to be faithful to what God has revealed to us about himself. In order to do that, we must use the correct words. Some people think that words do not matter. People of faith know otherwise. And the more we get to know God, the more we will know of God's love for us.

Do you remember the words of Saint John, "God is love"? How does it make you feel to know that the triune God loves you?

CATHOLIC ID

Catholics often refer to the "mysteries" of faith. A mystery is a truth of faith that we know only because God has revealed it to us. Human beings never fully understand a mystery. That is because only God, who is infinite, understands everything. However, it is the work of all believers to pray, study, and grow in understanding the mysteries of faith as much as they can. Think of this the next time you hear the words "Let us proclaim the mystery of faith" at Mass.

The Church and the Trinity

Almost everyone has heard the comparison of the Trinity to a shamrock, three leaves joined by one stem. This is certainly a clever way to approach the mystery of three in one. Another comparison is found in the legend of Saint Augustine at the seashore. According to the legend Augustine was watching a child trying to empty the vast ocean onto the shore, using a little sand bucket. When Augustine told the child that this was an impossible task, the child replied, "I'll finish this before you understand the Trinity."

Will we ever fully understand the Trinity? No. Otherwise we would be God. However, we have been privileged to get a glimpse of God's inner life. We are also privileged to live in relationship with God. The whole life of the Church, in fact, revolves around the Blessed Trinity. Catholics begin their prayers by making the sign of the cross. And the prayers of the liturgy are directed to God the Father, through the Son, in the Holy Spirit.

This is exactly what happens in the Mass and in the celebration of the sacraments. At Mass the eucharistic sacrifice of the Son is offered to the Father through the power of the Holy Spirit. Each of the sacraments also reminds us of the Trinity. Before a person is baptized, for example, he or she is asked to profess belief in the Father, Son, and Holy Spirit. Three questions are asked, one for each Person of the Trinity. These are the same questions we are asked each year on Easter when we renew our baptismal promises.

Speaking About the Trinity

What sets Christianity apart from every other religion is belief in the Blessed Trinity. The early Christians were accused by some of practicing polytheism. Muslims and Jews alike have taken offense at the doctrine of the Trinity. They feel that if God is three, then God cannot be one. Of course we know that Christians do not believe in three gods. We believe in the triune God, three Persons in the one God.

Sometimes people try to speak about the Blessed Trinity without using the words *Father* and *Son*. They are worried that we may be thinking of God only in masculine terms, which would be wrong. Instead of the Father, Son, and Holy Spirit, they prefer creator, redeemer, and sanctifier.

The words *creator*, *redeemer*, and *sanctifier* are the traditional words used to describe the roles and works of the Persons of the Blessed Trinity. It is true to say that the Father is the creator, the Son is the redeemer, and the Holy Spirit is the sanctifier. But using these words to replace the words *Father*, *Son*, and *Holy Spirit* can lead to misunderstanding. Why is that? Because *Father*, *Son*, and *Holy Spirit* are words that show us a relationship among the three divine Persons. The words *creator*, *redeemer*, and *sanctifier* are not words of relationship. Rather they refer to God's work of creating, redeeming, and sanctifying; they do not tell us what God is. They are important but do not tell us about the inner life of God, which he has revealed to us.

What are we to think? It is important to remember that God is neither male nor female. God, who is spirit, has no gender. God's revelation to us, however, is clear: God is Father, Son, and Holy Spirit. We cannot change what God has told us.

Here is an easy way to remember and pray about this mystery of faith. Christians are baptized in the *name* of the Father and of the Son and of the Holy Spirit, not in their *names*. There is only one God, who is the Blessed Trinity.

Practice making the sign of the cross reverently so that it always will be a true profession of your belief in the Blessed Trinity.

Scripture UPDATE

When we call God Father, we are using the language of faith. This does not mean, however, that we cannot describe God with feminine images. In Scripture God is compared to a mother. In Isaiah 66:13, for example, God says, "As a mother comforts her son, so will I comfort you."

Three interlocking rings is a symbol of the Trinity

PUTTING IT TOGETHER

things to think about

Were you surprised to find out that God alone is holy? What does this belief mean to you?

Imagine that you received a message in your E-mail one day that read, "Words do not make a difference in the life of faith." Your response?

things to share

Imagine that a non-Christian friend wants to know what Christians mean by the Blessed Trinity. What will you say?

A fourth-century Father of the Church, Saint Gregory of Nazianzus, wrote: "Above all guard for me this great deposit of faith, for which I live and fight, which I want to take with me as a companion…: I mean the profession of faith in the Father and the Son and the Holy Spirit. I entrust it to you today." What will you do with this great treasure entrusted to you?

WORDS TO REMEMBER

Find and define the following:

Blessed Trinity_____

_____

_____

transcendence_____

_____

_____

OnLine WITH THE PARISH

Each time you attend Mass, listen carefully for the words of the Eucharistic Prayer:
Through him,
with him,
in him,
in the unity of the Holy Spirit,
all glory and honor is yours,
almighty Father,
for ever and ever.

Your firm response in the Great Amen will be a wonderful example to others in your parish family of your belief in the Blessed Trinity.

What are some of the images used by Isaiah to share his experience of the transcendent God?

1

Are angels like God or like human beings? Explain.

2

What do we mean when we say that the three Persons in one God are distinct from one another?

3

Why was Arius wrong in his teachings about the Blessed Trinity?

4

Why is the doctrine of the Blessed Trinity the central teaching of the Christian religion?

5

Life in the Spirit

In your personal prayer this week, focus on the first words of the Lord's Prayer: "Our Father, who art in heaven, hallowed be thy name." Say the words slowly, and let them lead you into a deeper awareness of God's transcendence and God's immanence.

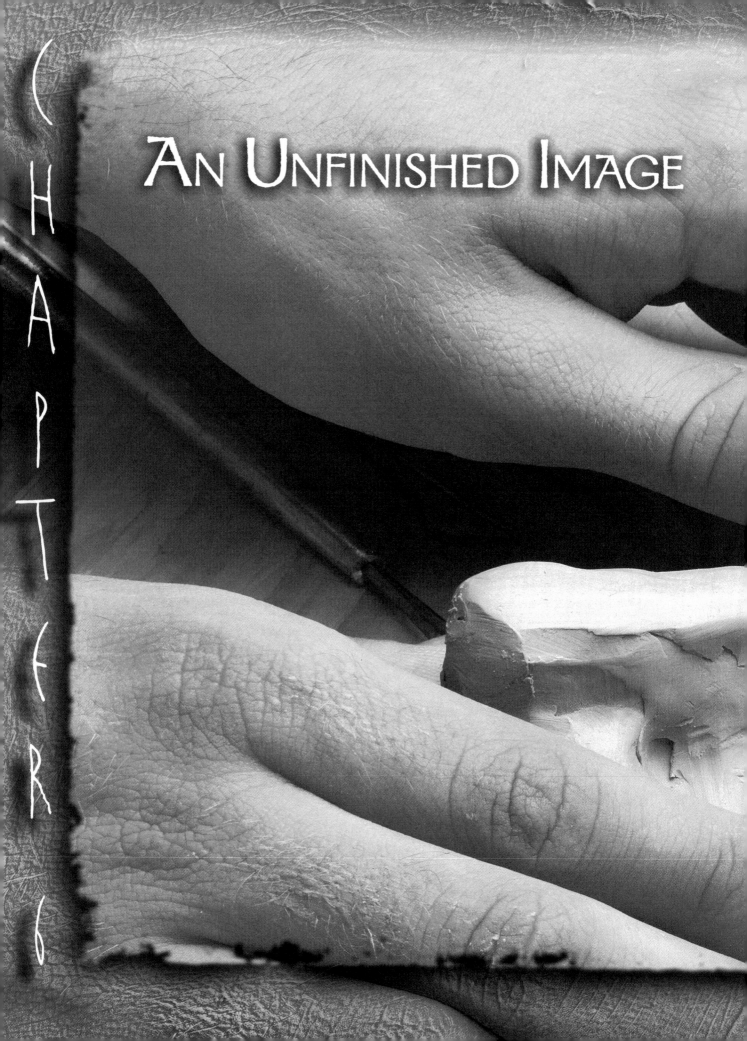

AN UNFINISHED IMAGE

CHAPTER 6

I praise you,
so wonderfully you made me;
wonderful are your works!

Psalm 139: 14

ON Ash Wednesday Christians have heard for centuries the words "Remember, you are dust, and to dust you will return." Dust! Is that all we are?

From the Dust of the Earth

Who are we? Where do we come from? Why are we here?

As people of faith we try to find out what God has revealed to us about human nature. It is important to discover not only what God has told us of himself but also what God has told us about ourselves. Because God is the source of all creation, the study of God and the study of the human person are like two sides of the same coin. We cannot study one without the other.

To help answer our questions, we turn to Genesis, which gives us the basis for our vision of human nature. Under the inspiration of the Holy Spirit,

the Genesis writers taught two important truths: that men and women are made in the image of God and that every human being has an immortal soul. These are the most basic truths that God revealed about us.

In God's Image The first mention of humankind in Genesis is truly simple. It is that God created human beings in his image: "God created man in his image; in the divine image he created him; male and female he created them" (Genesis 1:27). Men and women were made in God's image. What does this mean?

The phrase *in God's image* tells us several important things. First, it tells us that God created Adam and Eve—the names of the first people in the Genesis story—as his friends. God shared the gift of divine life with them and with no other creatures on earth. Second, the phrase *in God's image* tells us that human beings were created with an intellect and a will. Like God we are intelligent beings; we can think and are free to choose.

Unlike plants and animals, human beings can know and love God. This is the reason we were created. And what is important to understand is that we know and love God freely. We are not forced. With this freedom we can choose to grow in the divine image in which we were created. Or we can choose to remain unfinished images.

After teaching this startling truth about our human nature, the second chapter of Genesis continues with a symbolic and wonderfully imaginative description of humanity's creation. The biblical writers picture God as a sculptor forming the first human being from the dust of the earth, shaping clay and breathing life into it.

As strange as this poetic imagery may seem to modern, scientific minds, it should not be surprising. It was really based on the experience of ancient people. When they saw a dead body decay and turn to dust, they concluded that the human body was made and shaped from dust, the very elements of the earth. This may seem obvious, but it contains an extraordinary truth about human beings: Our bodies are made out of the same elements as the rest of creation. That connects us closely with the world around us and gives us reason to live as its responsible keepers.

An Immortal Soul   The Genesis writers pictured God the sculptor as putting his own life and breath into the first human being. Again, this was not a strange image for ancient peoples. After all, when a person stopped breathing, that person was dead. Breath meant life, as it does for us today. Just think of mouth-to-mouth resuscitation.

What did the biblical writers mean by the breath of life? In later times people thought of it as the soul. The *soul* is the spiritual part of every person; each of us has a soul created by God. Unlike the body, the soul has no parts. It is spiritual; it cannot die. That is why the soul is immortal.

Is the soul better than the body? Not really. We are a unity; we are body and soul. This is a truth that science cannot give us. This is a truth that only faith can provide.

Being an unfinished image isn't bad. It just means that we have to grow in God's image. What do you think the biggest challenge is in doing this?

form of animal life. On the other hand Catholics believe that this was done according to a plan set in motion by the creator. Human beings are not simply the result of chance.

Scientists draw their conclusions from studying ancient civilizations and the remains of past human life. They also examine fossils found in different layers of the earth. All these studies give scientists reliable evidence that the human race has evolved over the centuries. Catholics respect this evidence.

When Catholics talk about the evolution of the human race, they are referring only to the body, never to the soul. Through science we know that the body is made up of material parts that can develop and evolve. But the soul is spiritual. It has no material parts and therefore is not subject to development and evolution.

Science, however, is not concerned with the study of the soul. Science leaves that to religion and theology. The Church teaches that God creates each human soul directly and immediately. The soul is not produced by parents. Unlike the human body, the soul is not the result of biological reproduction. It is spiritual and without parts. The soul is the result of a divine act, a direct act of God.

Catholics and Evolution

Everyone is interested in the question of human origins. The topic is a concern of both religion and science. It is therefore important to know the truths about human origins found in the Bible and how they stack up against the findings of science.

To explain creation scientists speak of evolution. *Evolution* is a scientific theory; it states that higher forms of life evolved from lower forms of life. This theory has nothing to do with the truth of faith that God created everything. Nor does it upset the truth that we are a special part of God's creation.

Why is this so? Science and religion ask different kinds of questions; they look at the same truth from different points of view. On the one hand there is strong scientific evidence to support the theory that the human body evolved from a lower

CATHOLIC TEACHINGS

About the Unity of Humanity

The creation of human beings as described in Genesis gives the basis for the Church's teaching about the unity of humanity: "Because of its common origin *the human race forms a unity*, for 'from one ancestor [God] made all nations to inhabit the whole earth'" (*Catechism*, 360). Catholics who take this teaching seriously can never participate in prejudice of any kind. People of every time and place are members of the same human race, and each person's soul is created directly by God.

Science and Faith

For Catholics there is no clash or conflict between Church teachings and what science tells us about evolution. Both are meant to bring us to the truth, and the truth is one. Thus Catholics may and do accept the theory that the human body evolved.

If you stop to think about it, we actually take evolution for granted in our everyday speech. We do not go around saying, "God created that rock, that tree, that river"—not directly, that is. God created in the beginning, and his creative act now works out according to the laws of nature that he put into matter at the dawn of creation. That includes our bodies. It is only the human soul that God must create directly.

Why is it so important to understand all these details about science and faith? Today some people rely only on science to answer life's mysteries and to solve all problems. This "science only" point of view is narrow-minded because it fails to recognize that the human person is both material and spiritual, body and soul. Science takes into account only the material part of humanity.

The real answers to the meaning of life take into account the whole human person, not just one part. That is why it is necessary to accept what we find in Scripture, as it is taught by the Church, together with the findings of science.

Some people go to the opposite extreme, however. They place their trust only in the Bible and ignore the insights of scientific study. Such a viewpoint is equally narrow-minded because it is based on a literal understanding of the Bible unacceptable to Catholics. As we saw in an earlier chapter, the Church teaches that the creation language of Genesis is richly symbolic. Taking it literally robs God of his attributes and forces upon God the limitations of a human artisan. A literal interpretation fails to recognize the splendor of God's intelligence and power that lies behind the process of evolution. Who but God could create in such an elaborate and magnificent way?

Someone tells you that you cannot accept the idea of evolution if you believe in the Bible. As a Catholic what is the first thing you would want to share with that person?

Archaeological dig

69

Sin and Grace

Like everything in creation, the human race was created good. "God looked at everything he had made, and he found it very good" (Genesis 1:31). Made in God's image, human beings were given a share in God's own life at creation. This share in God's life we call sanctifying grace. *Sanctifying grace* is a participation in the very life of God that brings us into an intimate and permanent relationship with the Blessed Trinity. We first receive this divine gift at Baptism.

The idea of sanctifying grace is presented symbolically in the second and third chapters of Genesis. Adam and Eve are described as being in a beautiful garden, living in perfect happiness. There they had an easy friendship and personal relationship with God. This means that they were in the state of grace; they recognized their dependence on God and freely gave God their respect and trust. Then they were tested and given an opportunity to show their love for God. But by choosing freely to disobey him, our first parents proved themselves incredibly ungrateful for all that God had planned for them.

By disobeying God, Adam and Eve committed the first sin of humanity. We call this original sin. *Original sin* was the rejection of God by our first parents, resulting in the loss of sanctifying grace. With their sin Adam and Eve deprived themselves and all their descendants of the original state of grace given by God.

Down through the ages people have often referred to the sin of our first parents as "Adam's sin." So serious and deep was the wound of Adam's sin that it affected the whole human race. In the Genesis story Adam was the whole of humanity, along with Eve; and when he sinned, all humanity sinned in and with him. Thus all human beings are born in the state of original sin. Saint Paul was referring to humanity's sin through Adam when he wrote that just as "through one person sin entered the world, and through sin, death," so death came to all of us because all sinned in Adam (Romans 5:12).

The Effects of Original Sin

Original sin was a rejection of God. The story of Adam and Eve's sin indicated their pride and refusal to obey God; they put their own desires and will before God's will. Their rejection of God's will ended with the loss of sanctifying grace, resulting in an emptiness and absence.

When we say that we are born with original sin, we are not talking about a personal sin we have committed. We mean that we are born without sanctifying grace. We share the same emptiness and absence of grace that all humanity has suffered since the sin of our first parents. That is the reason the Church teaches that infants are to be baptized as soon as possible. Baptism restores us to the original state of grace given to humanity.

Besides losing sanctifying grace, our first parents lost other privileges when they sinned. From the Genesis story we know that the whole human race is forever subject to the following effects of original sin:

- *Ignorance:* As everyone knows, learning does not always come easily.
- *Suffering:* Suffering and pain are part of life. We cannot escape them.
- *Inclination to evil:* Like Adam and Eve we are tempted to see evil as good and are tempted to reject God.
- *Death:* Because of sin, human beings cannot escape death, either.

Scripture UPDATE

Scripture sometimes refers to "fallen angels" or "the devil." In 2 Peter 2:4 we read that "God did not spare the angels when they sinned." In 1 John 3:8 we read, "Whoever sins belongs to the devil, because the devil has sinned from the beginning." The Church's tradition understands in these references the existence of fallen angels, who embraced evil by their own doing. Such beings are creatures only and have no power over God.

As members of the human race, we inherit the effects of Adam's sin. This is a great mystery. Although we are not personally responsible for Adam's sin, each one of us who sins agrees with the choice of Adam. We, too, freely and personally join Adam in his rebellion against God.

We often refer to the free decision of Adam and Eve to turn away from God as "the fall." The free choice that was made by the first human beings to sin against God resulted in a "fallen" human nature. The human race has fallen from the close relationship with God that God first intended for us. In this fallen state, however, humanity is not totally lost. Human nature has been wounded and weakened but did not become totally evil or totally corrupted. God's creation is still good, but it is in need of a share in the divine life, in need of sanctifying grace.

Make a list of some current events that might help to explain the Church's teaching on original sin.

Can you name some effects of original sin?

71

God's Promise

There are some people in the world who do not believe in sin at all, much less original sin. They try to explain it away. But they cannot do so, not if they are honest. All they have to do is look at the evening news on television or read the daily paper. The results of original sin are all around us. We are far from being perfect creatures, and this certainly makes original sin an easy doctrine to accept.

If human beings freely chose to commit original sin at the dawn of human history, then humanity itself is the cause of sin and evil in the world. God is not the cause of evil. He created everything good. God did not force the first human beings to commit sin. It was their free choice to disobey their creator. Human beings are the ones who have turned good into evil by their own choice. This is a revealed truth of our faith.

Is humanity therefore without hope? Is fallen human nature beyond repair?

Some people have held that it is, but that is not the Catholic view. The Church teaches that even though human beings abused their freedom by choosing to sin, God did not abandon them. This is clearly seen in the story of Adam and Eve as it unfolds in the third chapter of Genesis. According to that account our first parents were tempted by a serpent, the symbol of evil, to disobey God. Adam and Eve chose disobedience. But before God expelled them from the garden, a symbol of their loss of sanctifying grace, he held out a promise to them. That promise is contained in a statement that God made to the serpent, the tempter:

> I will put enmity between you and the woman,
>   and between your offspring and hers;
> He will strike at your head,
>   while you strike at his heel.
> Genesis 3:15

What does this statement mean? Catholics have understood it as the first promise of salvation given by God. As we look at this verse, we are able to see the fulfillment of God's promise in Jesus. The reason for this is that we have the advantage of reading this promise from a New Testament point of view. It is not difficult to look back now to the opening chapters of Genesis and read into them what we know: that Jesus' passion, death, and resurrection brought the saving victory over sin and evil. Evil would not have the last word.

Statue of Christ the Redeemer
overlooking Rio de Janeiro, Brazil

Just as Jesus is referred to as the "new Adam," the Blessed Virgin Mary has been called the "new Eve." The Fathers of the Church saw in Mary's obedience the exact opposite of Eve's disobedience. Because Mary's son brought new life to the world, she has been called the mother of the living.

A Promise of Hope

What about the woman mentioned in the verse? Obviously it is Eve. But Catholics also think of another woman when they read Genesis 3:15. We think of Mary, the mother of Jesus, as the woman whose offspring would put his "heel" on the serpent and crush its "head." What a beautiful and hope-filled promise we have in this verse! It has often been called the first announcement of the good news of salvation.

Scripture and tradition picture Jesus as the "new Adam," who overcame the faults of the first Adam. Instead of the emptiness and absence of grace left to us by Adam, Jesus, the new Adam, brings us an overflow of divine life and grace. As Saint Paul wrote, "For just as in Adam all die, so too in Christ shall all be brought to life" (1 Corinthians 15:22).

One of the great truths of our faith is that human beings are good even though we are flawed by original sin. Original sin did not make human nature evil but did weaken it. As a result we have to work constantly against the effects of original sin in our lives. These include fear, jealousy, pride, selfishness—all the things that make human beings less than what God created us to be. And this struggle will continue our whole lives, even with the help of God's grace. The doctrine of original sin, therefore, is not only about something that happened a long time ago. It also tells us about ourselves today.

Even with original sin we are still loved by God. And human beings have been given almost unimaginable capabilities. Think of the wonderful things we can do, what great thoughts we can think. We have even landed on the moon! And what is most exciting, we have been called to participate in God's very life. What a marvelous creature is a human being that God would even think to become one of us at the incarnation!

Give an example for the following statement: Even though human beings have been weakened by original sin, we are still good.

things
to think about

Perhaps you have seen bumper stickers that read, "Be patient. God isn't finished with me yet." Name three ways in which you will cooperate with God in developing his unfinished image in you.

Then consider what you have learned about the Catholic view of human nature. Is it more fitting for a Catholic to be an optimist or a pessimist about life?

things
to share

Some people say that the evolution of the human body is a terrible idea because it contradicts the Bible. What will you say to these people about the Catholic view of evolution?

A family you know is about to celebrate the Baptism of a new baby. The parents have a problem with the idea of original sin. They say to you, "It's unfair. Our baby never did anything wrong." Your response?

WORDS TO REMEMBER

Find and define the following:

sanctifying grace: _____
_____
_____

original sin: _____
_____
_____

OnLine
WITH THE PARISH

Catholics who take seriously the Church's teaching about the unity of humanity are always aware of the evil of racial prejudice. Brainstorm with your group several ways you can campaign against prejudice in speech or in action. Then discuss ways you will share your campaign ideas with the rest of your parish.

What do we mean when we say that each person has an immortal soul? Explain.

1

What is the Catholic position on human evolution?

2

How did the Genesis writers present in a symbolic way the idea of sanctifying grace?

3

Why are all people born in the state of original sin?

4

Name one effect of original sin and explain it.

5

Life in the Spirit

In her prayer journal a Catholic teen wrote, "Dear God: I now realize that the more I come to know you, the more I come to know myself. Help me to recognize your image in me." Centuries ago Saint Augustine prayed, "Let me know you, O you who know me; let me know you, as I am known." Reflect on the meaning of these prayers. Compose a similar prayer from your own heart.

For my eyes have seen your salvation,
a light for revelation to the Gentiles,
and glory for your people Israel.

Luke 2:30, 32

THERE are no photographs of him. He never wrote a book or traveled far from the place where he was born. Yet he is supposed to be the center of our lives. This is Jesus of Nazareth. What do we know about him?

Nazareth today

The Fullness of Time

It was the fullness of time. The Roman Empire stretched from Spain and Britain in the west to Palestine and Syria in the east. It was a time of peace, with law and order assured by Roman soldiers stationed throughout the empire. For the first time in human history, good roads went everywhere. Never before had so many nations been united in one empire.

There was still unrest, however. Many of the proud peoples from different countries and cultures of the Roman Empire hated the foreign forces that occupied their lands. In Palestine the Jews were especially unhappy. King Herod, a Jew, had been appointed by Rome, but he was not the king the Jews wanted, one from the line of King David.

Instead they looked forward even more toward the coming of the Messiah, the promised one. Some thought he would be a great military leader who would protect them from their enemies and expel the hated foreign invaders. There was restlessness in the air. And then the time arrived. "When the fullness of time had come, God sent his Son, born of a woman" (Galatians 4:4).

Jesus was born without any display or fanfare. Mary was his virgin mother; and Joseph, his foster father, was a descendant of King David. Mary and Joseph had gone to the little town of Bethlehem to be registered in the Roman census. Every citizen of the empire had to register so that the emperor would have an accurate count for tax purposes. It was in Bethlehem that Jesus was born. In the great empire of Rome, he was just another statistic in the census.

After eight days the child born of Mary was named Jesus. The name *Jesus* means "God saves." Very little is known of Jesus' childhood and early life in Nazareth. Luke sums it up in one verse: "Jesus advanced in wisdom and age and favor before God and man" (Luke 2:52).

Even though we have no record of his childhood, we do know from many sources what life must have been like at the time of Jesus. Like the other boys of Nazareth, Jesus probably attended the local synagogue school. It seems clear that he did not set himself apart from the other young people of his town. He was not wealthy. He grew up just as everyone else did.

When Jesus was about thirty years old and ready to begin his public preaching, people barely noticed him. As he approached John the Baptist to be baptized in the Jordan River, John told the crowd, "There is one among you whom you do not recognize" (John 1:26). But John recognized Jesus! So John pointed to him and said, "Behold, the Lamb of God, who takes away the sin of the world" (John 1:29). With these words John the Baptist was comparing Jesus to the lamb used at Passover: Jesus was to shed his blood like a sacrificial lamb.

John's baptism was not like the sacrament of Baptism we have today. It was a ritual of repentance, a sign that people wanted to change their lives. Although Jesus had no need of repentance, he asked for John's baptism. In this way Jesus would identify himself with the rest of humanity. Then, at the moment of baptism, a startling event took place:

"On coming up out of the water he [Jesus] saw the heavens being torn open and the Spirit, like a dove, descending upon him. And a voice came from the heavens, 'You are my beloved Son; with you I am well pleased'" (Mark 1:10–11).

It might appear from Mark's Gospel that everyone present at Jesus' baptism heard a voice from heaven and saw the Holy Spirit descend upon Jesus. That is not so. Jesus alone saw and heard the heavenly happenings. In that moment he was set apart for his ministry, his Father's work. During the rest of his life on earth, Jesus would gradually reveal himself as both God and Man.

If you were an artist, how would you picture Jesus? How would you want people to see him?

Jesus pictured as the Lamb of God on an ivory book cover

*Detail from **Coronation of the Virgin**, Diego Rodriguez Velazquez, 1641–1642*

In the Beginning

At the very heart and life of Christian faith is Jesus of Nazareth. He is the most unique individual in human history. Why is this so? To answer this question, Christians turn to the earliest communities who knew Jesus and were closest to him. What do they tell us about his coming to our world? Most talk about his birth at Bethlehem, using wonderful stories of faith to help us understand him. But one gospel in particular gets right to the core of Jesus' identity in a way unlike any other. This is the Gospel of John, in which Jesus is called the "Word," who came to earth to live with us.

The *Word* is the name for the second Person of the Blessed Trinity in Saint John's Gospel. Why did John use this name, the *Word*? He was reminding us of a wonderful truth: that through words we express the deepest part of ourselves. This is true of God as well. By calling the second Person of the Trinity the *Word*, John was telling us that the Word is the deepest expression of God himself. In John's Gospel we read:

> In the beginning was the Word,
> and the Word was with God,
> and the Word was God.
> John 1:1

In three simple clauses John tells us three important truths:

- The Word, the second Person of the Blessed Trinity, always existed; the Word was already there at the start of creation.
- The Word was present with God but was distinct from him. (Remember, the Son is not the Father.)
- The Word was divine. The Word was distinct from God, but the Word was also God, sharing the same divine nature.

Later in the first chapter of John's Gospel we read, "And the Word became flesh and made his dwelling among us" (John 1:14). In this verse John tells us that the Word came to earth to live *with us*. John had already told us about the Word's divinity, that the Word was *God*. Here John speaks of the Word as *human*. The Word has become flesh, a frail mortal, taking on a human nature like our own.

The Incarnation

The taking on of flesh by the Word is not an easy idea to understand. As used by John, *Word* refers to a "Person," to the God-Man Jesus Christ. God reveals himself to us in this Word. Jesus is God's message to us in the flesh.

To describe this great event, we talk about the *incarnation*, a word meaning "the putting on or taking on of flesh." Christians define the *incarnation* as the union of divinity with humanity

CATHOLIC ID Ignatius of Antioch, one of the Fathers of the Church, taught clearly about the humanity of Jesus. In A.D. 110 he wrote, "Do not listen when anyone speaks to you apart from Jesus Christ, who was of the race of David, who was the son of Mary, who was truly born and ate and drank, was truly persecuted under Pontius Pilate, was truly crucified and died" (*Letter to the Trallians*, 9).

in Jesus Christ. It is the mystery of the second Person of the Blessed Trinity becoming one of us, the mystery of Jesus Christ being God and Man. Jesus is the Word of God made flesh.

There is a great deal to think about here. Jesus is truly divine and truly human. He is not God disguised as a human or God wearing a human mask. Jesus is one of us, with a human soul and body like ours. To all who knew him in Galilee and Judaea, he was the man Jesus. He got hungry and thirsty; he grew tired. Sometimes he was happy, sometimes sad. He knew fear, loneliness, and discouragement. He perspired in the heat and shivered in the cold. He went fishing and got his hands dirty. He was one of us in all things except

this: He was sinless. Nevertheless, in becoming fully human, he did not stop being God. That is why the early Church could proclaim, "He is the image of the invisible God" (Colossians 1:15), the perfect image of the Father.

Although this teaching of the Church about the incarnation is very clear today, it was not always so. Some Christians in the early Church held that Jesus only *appeared* to be human. They said that it was unworthy of God to become incarnate with a human body and to live, suffer, and die.

Today we know that these people were wrong. The Church teaches that Jesus *was truly* a man. He did not *just appear* to be a man. He was not God in a human disguise. That is why a New Testament writer could truthfully say that he had heard, had seen with his own eyes, and had touched with his hands the Word of life (1 John 1:1–3).

Do you think people need to know more about Jesus' divinity or his humanity? Explain.

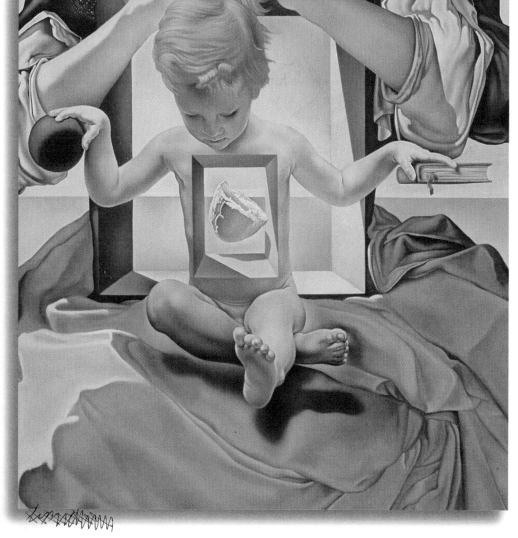

Detail from **Madonna of Port Lligat**, 1950. Salvador Dalí's symbolic representation of the incarnation reminding us that Jesus is the Bread of Life.

Jesus of Nazareth

What can we possibly know about Jesus of Nazareth, who lived two thousand years ago? Did he really exist? As people of faith our answer is, "Of course!" Nevertheless nonbelievers may say, "What proof do you have?"

What would your answer to that question be? Are the faith statements we call the New Testament our only source of knowing whether or not Jesus even existed? The answer is no. There are a number of ancient historical sources that verify and support the existence of Jesus.

In Josephus   One of the most famous nonbiblical sources that refers to Jesus comes from a Jewish historian who died at the end of the first century. His name was Flavius Josephus. Here is what he wrote about Jesus and his followers:

> At this time there appeared Jesus, a wise man…. For he was a doer of startling deeds, a teacher of people who received the truth with pleasure. And he gained a following both among many Jews and among many of Greek origin…. And when Pilate, because of an accusation made by the leading men among us, condemned him to the cross, those who had loved him previously did not cease to do so…. And up until this very day the tribe of Christians, named after him, has not died out.
> *Antiquities of the Jews*, vol. 18

In Tacitus   Among several pagan Roman writers, we can read the words of the Roman historian Tacitus. He wrote about the great fire in Rome during the reign of the emperor Nero in A.D. 64. Nero was afraid of rumors that he had set the great fire himself. Tacitus wrote:

> To squelch the rumor, Nero created scapegoats and subjected to the most refined tortures those whom the common people called "Christians," hated for their abominable crimes. Their name comes from Christ, who, during the reign of Tiberius, had been executed by the procurator Pontius Pilate. Suppressed for the moment, the deadly superstition broke out again, not only in Judaea, the land which originated this evil, but also in the city of Rome.
> *Annals*, 15, 44

There is no doubt that when Tacitus wrote these words in A.D. 115 he was not a lover of Christianity, since he calls it an evil and a superstition. He certainly knows about the place from which Christianity comes and about its founder. However, from Tacitus, as well as from Josephus and other nonbiblical writers, it is clear that Jesus was not simply an idea dreamed up by someone.

*Scripture*UPDATE

One of the shortest verses in Scripture eloquently describes the humanity of Jesus. It does so in three words: "And Jesus wept" (John 11:35). Jesus had just gone to see the burial place of his friend Lazarus. Jesus' love for his friend was so great that he cried. What deeper expression of human emotion is there?

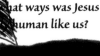
In what ways was Jesus human like us?

In the Gospels Our most valuable sources for information about Jesus of Nazareth are the gospel accounts. Of course they were never meant to be like modern history textbooks. But they are based on what really happened in history. The gospels are important because they give us the meaning of this history for our faith.

From the gospels we learn that Jesus grew up in Nazareth of Galilee and was known as the Nazarene. People were not amazed at his unusual abilities: As a baby he did not talk in the manger; as a child he did not work miracles. He had to grow in knowledge as we do. He did not have automatic answers to life's problems. Despite what some people or some artists might envision, Jesus had not been a full-grown man living in heaven from all eternity who shrank into a baby before entering Mary's womb.

Growing up in the Galilean hills, Jesus had to learn many things about life. Although he was a carpenter by trade, his speech and understanding of life were influenced by the farming communities of the area and all that farmers experience. He knew about vineyards and growing grapes, as well as about the daily wages of farmers.

When Jesus was sick, he had to take medicine and rest. He enjoyed being with his friends and no doubt engaged in the sports of his day. Without a telephone, television, or computer, Jesus learned many things from listening to his family, relatives, and the people of the village as they discussed the problems of everyday life. Jesus even had to learn how to pray. When we look at the life of Jesus of Nazareth, we see that he lived a normal life.

Are you surprised to find out that Jesus had to learn how to pray? What does this fact tell you about being a follower of Jesus?

Jesus the Man

When it happened, we do not know exactly. But one day Jesus left his hometown of Nazareth and began what we now call his public life. It was time for him to bring the good news to others. So he set out on a journey throughout Palestine. This journey, however, was not going to be a long one. It would last only about three years.

The gospel accounts of Matthew, Mark, Luke, and John are for the most part concerned with the public life and message of Jesus, what he did and what he said. If we take these gospels and put them together, we can begin to draw a sketch of the man Jesus. Certainly the gospels do not provide us with everything there is to know about him; this was not their purpose. But they do give us a definite impression of Jesus' life and the kind of individual he was.

During the years of his public life, Jesus made many friends—and enemies, too. But no matter what people may have thought of him, Jesus was an exciting and impressive individual. Here was a man who had come to know what life was all about. Those who believed in him and followed him found a new purpose in living. They said, "Never before has anyone spoken like this one" (John 7:46).

Likable   The gospels clearly picture Jesus as a likable friend, searching people out. Wherever people were, he went to them: their homes, the streets, the marketplace. Jesus did not keep a distance from others but was involved in their everyday lives. That is why he attended wedding feasts, banquets, and other gatherings to which he was invited.

Jesus must have been easy to talk with. He shared himself with his friends, as all friends do. He rejoiced with them when things were going well, wept with them when they were sad. He visited their homes and sometimes stayed overnight, as he did with Zacchaeus (Luke 19:1–10). No one was a stranger to Jesus. His friends included the rich and the poor, the young and the old, the popular and

Laughing Jesus,
Nuñez Segura, 1988

the unpopular. He knew shepherds and how they felt looking for a stray sheep. He could sympathize with a housewife who had lost some money.

Jesus went out of his way for those who were sick or in need, even for those who were outcasts and hated by others. Though Jesus was compassionate,

Galilee today

And with the Twelve, Jesus was a thoughtful friend, too. Once, after the apostles had spent a full day on the road, Jesus invited them to take a break. He said, "Come away by yourselves to a deserted place and rest a while" (Mark 6:31).

With his disciples gathered close to him, Jesus was filled with joy and sought out those who were thought to be "lost." Some people complained about him, "This man welcomes sinners and eats with them" (Luke 15:2). But these sinners were the ones with whom Jesus wanted to spend his time; they were the ones who needed him most.

Jesus also treated women differently than was customary. Unlike other teachers Jesus welcomed women among his followers. Together with the Twelve some women accompanied Jesus on his travels (Luke 8:1–3). Still others were taught by Jesus, as Martha and Mary were (Luke 10:38–42).

This gospel sketch of Jesus shows us a man who came to know exactly who he was. Full of love, Jesus was ready to face anything in life. He was fully alive and fully human. But this is only half the story. As the incarnation reminds us, he was also divine, the Son of God.

 Which gospel passage helps you to remember that Jesus is your friend, too?

he was not a weakling. Discouraged at times, he never gave up. Rejected, he went back to his task again and again. Hated, he loved in return. Not that he was without feeling. He had moments of anger (Matthew 21:12–13) and loneliness, too.

Concerned for Everyone To those who followed him, Jesus spoke boldly about God's place in their lives. He called them to be his disciples and to turn to God. One of the things we can admire most in the man Jesus is his strong determination. He was misunderstood by many but never changed what he knew he had to do or say. Even in the face of opposition, he continued to teach with authority.

Perhaps the best way we can identify with Jesus as a friend is to see the way he treated people. He enjoyed them. Somehow we can tell when others like us. The apostles felt that same warmth with Jesus. With little hesitation they decided to join him (Mark 1:16–20) and became the Twelve.

CATHOLIC TEACHINGS

About Jesus' Humanity

The Church never wants us to forget that Jesus was a Jew. He was born into a Jewish family and grew up practicing the Jewish religion. He cherished the traditions of his ancestors and worshiped God in the local synagogue and at the Temple in Jerusalem. To forget that Jesus was a Jew is to forget an essential part of his humanity.

PUTTING IT TOGETHER

things to think about

Someone says to you, "Jesus could never know what it's like to be me or know how I feel. Besides, he had all the answers. He didn't have to work at anything!" What is your response as a Catholic?

things to share

A recent drawing of Jesus shows him laughing and having fun. Some people think that it might be disrespectful to show Jesus this way. What would you say about it?

WORDS TO REMEMBER

Find and define the following:

the Word _____

_____

_____

incarnation _____

_____

_____

OnLine
WITH THE PARISH

The gospels portray Jesus as a true and loving friend, someone who was concerned about others. How can you imitate the concern of Jesus by helping out in your parish community? Find out what helping organizations exist in your parish. Then discover how you might become a part of their ministry.

What do we mean when we speak of Jesus coming among us in the fullness of time?

1

How do we know that Jesus really existed?

2

Where do we get our information about the public life of Jesus? Explain.

3

Why is it wrong to say that Jesus only *appeared* to be a human?

4

How did Jesus relate to the men and women of his time?

5

Life in the Spirit

Take a few moments this week to do your own gospel sketch of Jesus. Choose any of the four gospel accounts. Then make a list of all the wonderful human qualities you see in Jesus our friend and brother. Use this list as your own litany of thanksgiving to Jesus. For example, you might say, "Jesus, you cared for those in need. Help me to do the same."

CHAPTER 8

MESSIAH, LORD, AND SAVIOR

We adore you,
O Christ, and we praise you
because by your holy cross
you have redeemed the world.

WHAT was the purpose of Jesus' life?
Was he just a great teacher, a bearer of good news?
What difference has he made in our world?

Words Filled with Meaning

The birth of Jesus was like no other. That is why his coming was announced to shepherds by an angel who said, "Do not be afraid; for behold, I proclaim to you good news of great joy that will be for all the people. For today in the city of David a savior has been born for you who is Messiah and Lord" (Luke 2:10–11).

With a few simple words, Luke gives us a most important message about the meaning of Jesus' life: that he is Messiah, Lord, and Savior. What does each of these words mean?

Messiah   The word *messiah* is a Hebrew word meaning "anointed one." When this word was translated by the early Church into Greek, the word became *Christos*, or *Christ*. *Messiah* and *Christ*, therefore, mean the same thing.

Messiah was a very important word for God's people in Old Testament times. The word reminded them that priests, kings, and prophets were anointed with oil. When a king was enthroned, for example, oil was poured over his head. This meant that he was being set apart from all others and was responsible to God alone.

By the time of Jesus, there was no longer a king of Israel from the family of King David. Many people thought that the Messiah would come from that family as a king and warrior who would make Israel a great world power. Surely, they thought, this was God's promise to the chosen people.

Jesus, however, did not think this way. In fact he never called himself the Messiah. He did not want to give the impression that he agreed with the mistaken idea of the Messiah as a worldly king or warrior. For Jesus, the Messiah was to be a servant of God who would change the world by his suffering. The first Christians realized that Jesus was this Messiah, this suffering servant of God. They called him the Christ and therefore regarded Jesus as the true Messiah of Israel. Nevertheless, as Christianity spread throughout the world, other titles, such as "Lord" and "Savior," were used to describe who Jesus really was.

Lord   In Old Testament times the transcendent God, Yahweh, was referred to as the Lord. Using *Lord* for *Yahweh* was a sign of respect. So *Yahweh* (*God*) and *Lord* meant the same thing. Because Jesus was the Son of God—human and divine—he, too, was Lord. In fact the earliest expression of Christian faith was "Jesus Christ is Lord" (Philippians 2:11).

Savior   Just like the word *Lord*, the word *Savior* was used in the Old Testament to describe God. Because God rescued people from sin and death, he was frequently called Savior. We see this in the writings of the prophet Isaiah, for example. There God says, "For I am the LORD, your God, the Holy One of Israel, your savior" (Isaiah 43:3).

The work of the Savior is to bring salvation to the world. *Salvation* means "to heal," or "to be made whole." In Luke 2:10–11 Jesus, whose very name means "God saves," is announced to all as the Savior of the world. Jesus would restore the relationship that God had planned to share with humanity before original sin.

The salvation that Jesus gives is a healing from sin. It is sin that separates humanity from God. The goal of Jesus' life was to restore what God originally intended: that there be an intimate relationship between God and humanity and among people themselves. How could this be done? It would take someone who had the power of God to accomplish this, someone who was himself both God and Man. That Person was Jesus Christ our Lord.

 Jesus our Savior brings healing to the world. Where do you think Jesus' healing is most needed today?

A Divine Person

Throughout his life Jesus acted as someone with authority, doing what only God could do. The early Church professed its faith in this divinity of Jesus by saying "Jesus is the Son of God."

The people of Jesus' time knew that only God can forgive sins. No one but God can heal the break with God that sin causes in our lives. Nevertheless Jesus, the man from Nazareth, took it upon himself to forgive sins. He did this over and over again. In fact Jesus said that love of him wins forgiveness for sins. This was his message to the woman who showed great love for him. He said to her, "Your sins are forgiven" (Luke 7:48). This is the same message of love Jesus shares with us.

Jesus did other things that only a divine Person can do. One day some people tried to insult Jesus as he was speaking to them. When Jesus referred to Abraham in a close and familiar way, his listeners questioned him, saying, "You are not yet fifty years old and you have seen Abraham?" Jesus replied, "Amen, amen, I say to you, before Abraham came to be, I AM" (John 8:57, 58).

By calling himself I AM, Jesus was using the name God had revealed to Moses. When Moses had asked what God's name was, God said, "This is what you shall tell the Israelites: I AM sent me to you" (Exodus 3:14). By using the words I AM, Jesus was making himself an equal of Yahweh.

One day Jesus gave a glimpse of his divinity to the apostles Peter, James, and John at the transfiguration. In a brief moment Jesus' "face shone like the sun and his clothes became white as light." Then the apostles heard a voice saying, "This is my beloved Son, with whom I am well pleased; listen to him" (Matthew 17:2, 5). In this vision Jesus was letting his apostles know just how close he was with God the Father. At another time Jesus would tell the people, "The Father and I are one" (John 10:30).

Christ Redempteur, *Giraudon, 1393–94*

Worker of Miracles

The miracles of Jesus were signs of his divine power. Jesus raised the dead to life, gave sight to the blind, cured lepers, opened the ears of the deaf, enabled the lame to walk, and loosened the tongues of those who could not speak. Jesus also calmed the stormy sea and fed thousands on the hillside with just a few loaves of bread and pieces of fish.

Although Jesus worked many miracles, he did not make a show of his power. Filled with divine love and compassion, he even asked that his miraculous power be kept secret. One day a leper came to him. Calling Jesus "Lord," the leper asked to be cured. After Jesus cured him, he said to the leper, "See that you tell no one, but go show yourself to the priest, and offer the gift that Moses prescribed" (Matthew 8:4). Why did Jesus say this?

It was not out of a sense of false humility that Jesus asked for secrecy. He did not want people to become obsessed with the idea of power and think of him only as a miracle worker. Jesus wanted them to listen to his message. That is why he said, "Blessed are those who hear the word of God and observe it" (Luke 11:28).

 What do these words of Jesus tell you about being a disciple today?

The miracles of Jesus fill us with wonder, but they are not the cornerstones of our faith. Those who have faith in Jesus are able to believe in him only because faith is a God-given gift. It is true that miracles can lead people to believe, but they cannot produce faith. Faith is God's gift to those who freely accept his word. We accept God on his terms because it is God who is speaking.

CATHOLIC TEACHINGS

About the Person of Christ

In the early Church the following question arose: After the incarnation was Jesus two persons, a divine person and a human person? Or was he one person, and if so, a human person or a divine person? The followers of Nestorius, the bishop of Constantinople, mistakenly thought that Jesus was a human person in whom God was housed. This implied that Jesus was two persons: a divine person and a human person—like putting flowers in a vase (a divine person inside a human person).

To set things straight Nestorius himself asked that a Church council answer the question. The Council of Ephesus was called in A.D. 431. That council, as well as the Council of Chalcedon in A.D. 451, condemned any teaching that would split Christ into two persons. Ever since that time the Church has clearly taught that Jesus is one Person: a divine Person with two natures (a divine nature and a human nature). At the incarnation the second Person of the Trinity took on a human nature, not another person.

Christ of Saint John of the Cross, Dali, 1951

The Lamb of God

Although Jesus himself was sinless, he freely chose to take upon himself the sins of the world. That is why Jesus was willing to be condemned to death as a common criminal, to be crowned with thorns, and to carry his own cross to Calvary. His acceptance of his passion and death was a completely selfless act. "No one has greater love than this, to lay down one's life for one's friends" (John 15:13).

Because of his great love, Jesus was willing to die for us and to offer to God the sacrifice of his own life. Death was the result of sin, and Jesus met death head on. Because he embraced our human life totally, Jesus really experienced death and all the pain and sorrow that surround it. This was the perfect sacrifice, the only one that would reconcile humanity with God. Through his death and resurrection, Jesus enabled all people to pass over from death to a whole new life with God. This is what we call our redemption and why Jesus is our redeemer.

Sacrifice To understand what Jesus really did for us and for all humanity, we need to appreciate what it means to offer sacrifice. Offering a sacrifice does not mean that we deprive ourselves of

94

something. It is the offering of a gift. A *sacrifice* is a gift offered to God by a priest and destroyed in some way to show that it belongs to God alone. That is why the gift is burned or poured out or consumed. Offering a sacrifice is the highest form of worship that we can offer to God. How did this come to be?

Ancient people thought that blood was the force of life. In Old Testament times our ancestors in faith thought the same way. They offered an animal in sacrifice to praise God and show their sorrow for sin. This sacrificial victim was killed on an altar, and its blood was poured out. In this way the ancient Jews believed that they were offering the gift of life itself back to the Giver of life. It would be God's forever, never to be taken back. The sacrifice was followed by a sacrificial meal. To eat this meal was to be in communion with God, who accepted the sacrifice and came among the people as they shared it.

The Passover Sacrifice When offering a sacrifice, people gave only the best to God. They would offer their finest goat or calf, for example. At Passover an unblemished lamb was blessed and offered to God in sacrifice. The lamb was offered to God as a gift, as one of God's choicest creatures, both beautiful and innocent. Afterward all who shared in the Passover meal were united with one another and with Yahweh.

Passover was the celebration of Israel's "passing over" from slavery in Egypt to freedom, from death to life. During this celebration the Jews recalled all that God had done for them and God's saving and liberating activity in their history. At the first Passover it was the blood of the unblemished lamb that saved the firstborn children of Israel from death in Egypt. This made possible their departure for the promised land (Exodus 12:1–36).

Our Paschal Sacrifice Jesus Christ is our Savior. He is our paschal, or Passover, lamb offered in sacrifice to the Father. At the crucifixion on Calvary, it was his blood, the blood of the Lamb of God, that saved all people from the death of sin and freed them for the promised land of heaven.

Jesus was the paschal victim like no other. Through him salvation and forgiveness of sins came to the whole world. In Jesus "we have redemption by his blood" (Ephesians 1:7). In the one sacrifice of the Lamb of God, the sacrifices of the old covenant came to an end. Jesus was both priest and victim on the altar of the cross; "he entered once for all into the sanctuary, not with the blood of goats and calves but with his own blood, thus obtaining eternal redemption" (Hebrews 9:12).

In the Old Testament there were many sacrifices offered daily in the Temple. In the New Testament there is only one sacrifice—the sacrifice in Jesus' blood. We now share in this one sacrifice at Mass. Christ does not die at each Mass, for death no longer has a hold over him; he has passed from death to risen and glorified life. Nevertheless the Mass is truly a sacrifice; it re-presents (makes present for us again) the one sacrifice of Calvary, prolonged in time. It is a perfect sacrifice: The victim is Christ; the priest is Christ. "The same Christ who offered himself once in a bloody manner on the altar of the cross is contained and offered in an unbloody manner" in the sacrifice of the Mass (*Catechism*, 1367).

Now that you know more about sacrifice and Jesus' passion and death, which part of the Mass has greater meaning for you?

CATHOLIC ID

In reflecting upon the sacrifice of Jesus on the cross, the Church is reminded of the figure of the suffering servant. The prophet Isaiah described this servant as "pierced for our offenses" and taking upon himself "the guilt of us all." Isaiah also said that he was "like a lamb led to the slaughter" (Isaiah 53:5, 6, 7). That is why we call Jesus the Suffering Servant.

The New Covenant

Through Jesus' sacrifice on the cross, humanity has entered into a whole new relationship with God. We now have a new covenant established in the blood of Christ. What does this mean?

Long ago our ancestors in faith established a covenant, or agreement, with God on Mount Sinai. In this covenant they agreed to be God's chosen people, who would worship Yahweh as the one true God. Moses confirmed and sealed this covenant in Israel's name by sacrificing a lamb.

After the sacrifice was completed, Moses poured the lamb's blood on the altar. Then, following an ancient custom, he sprinkled some of the blood on the people assembled together. As he did this, he said, "This is the blood of the covenant which the LORD has made with you" (Exodus 24:8). Then the people ate the flesh of the lamb and were in communion with God and one another.

The covenant established at Sinai was the greatest event of the Old Testament. Through the laws of that covenant, God's people were formed and given life. The death and resurrection of Jesus are the greatest events in the New Testament. In them a new and everlasting covenant was confirmed and sealed, one that was made in Jesus' blood. Each time we participate in the Mass and share in the Body and Blood of Christ, the Lamb of God, we celebrate this new covenant and are in communion with God and one another.

Read again the words of Moses as he sprinkled the blood of the sacrificed lamb on the people. Now compare them with these words that we hear at each Mass: "Take this, all of you, and drink from it: this is the cup of my blood, the blood of the new and everlasting covenant. It will be shed for you and for all so that sins may be forgiven. Do this in memory of me." Both covenants were sealed in blood, but the new covenant was sealed in the blood of Christ.

Jesus, the Messiah, went beyond the expectations of all those around him. He rescued us from sin and brought salvation to everyone for all time. No one else could accomplish this. As we read in the Acts of the Apostles, "There is no salvation through anyone else, nor is there any other name under heaven given to the human race by which we are to be saved" (Acts 4:12).

The Resurrection

How can we be sure that the sacrifice of the cross brought us our salvation? We believe this because of Jesus' resurrection from the dead. As Paul declared, "If Christ has not been raised, then empty is our preaching; empty, too, your faith" (1 Corinthians 15:14). The resurrection is the main reason for our faith in Christ: It completes Christ's sacrifice of love on the cross.

What was Jesus' resurrection like? We know that it was a real event, a historical fact. But it was more than the miracles that Jesus worked. Remember Jesus' friend Lazarus, whom Jesus raised from the dead. Jesus was not brought back only to an earthly life like Lazarus, so that he would have to die again. Jesus' resurrection was different: He was raised to *new life*. What does this mean?

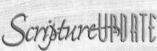

One of the most important titles for Jesus in the New Testament is Son of Man. In the gospel accounts this title is used only by Jesus when speaking of himself. Look up the following gospel passages in which *Son of Man* is used by Jesus, and see how rich and varied its many meanings are:

- Jesus referring to his human life (Luke 9:58)
- Jesus claiming divine powers (Mark 2:10)
- Jesus describing his mission (Luke 19:10)
- Jesus referring to his suffering and death (Mark 10:45)
- Jesus describing himself coming on the clouds of heaven as judge (Matthew 24:30–31). You may wish to read Daniel 7:13 in the Old Testament and compare both passages.

What will you think of the next time you hear *Son of Man* proclaimed at Mass?

This mystery of faith is never fully described in the gospels, but the testimony of eyewitnesses is clear. The risen Christ was seen and experienced by his followers. He ate with them and showed them his wounds. The risen body they saw was the same body that had been crucified and buried. Now risen, however, this real body had been totally transformed and was no longer subject to the laws of space and time. That is why the risen Jesus could pass through locked doors. In the gospels he is described as suddenly entering a locked room (John 20:19). We call the risen and transformed body of Christ his glorified body.

 What does it mean for you to know that the risen Christ is with us today?

things to think about

Why do you think Saint Paul said that our faith would be empty if Christ had not risen from the dead?

Why do you think that Jesus, the Messiah, did not make a show of his miraculous power?

WORDS TO REMEMBER

Find and define the following:

Savior _____

_____

_____

sacrifice _____

_____

_____

things to share

Share with your family and friends why it is so important for Christians to know about the Jewish Passover, the paschal lamb, the covenant at Sinai, and the offering of sacrifice. What do all these have to do with our salvation in Jesus Christ?

OnLine WITH THE PARISH

Arrange for your group to go on a "field trip" to your parish church. You will want to look especially at the altar, the vestments, and the sacred vessels used at the sacrifice of the Mass. See whether you can find any symbols that remind you of Jesus, the Lamb of God.

What do we mean when we say that Jesus, our Savior, brings us salvation?

1

Can the miracles of Jesus produce faith in us? Why or why not?

2

Why did Jesus have to die on the cross for us?

3

Why do we say that the one sacrifice of Jesus established a new and an everlasting covenant with God?

4

Explain the difference between the resurrection of Jesus and the resurrection of Lazarus.

5

Life in the Spirit

At each Mass we say or sing,

Lamb of God, you take away
    the sins of the world:
    have mercy on us.
Lamb of God, you take away
    the sins of the world:
    have mercy on us.
Lamb of God, you take away
    the sins of the world:
    grant us peace.

Spend a few moments thinking about these words. Then make up your own prayer to Jesus, our paschal lamb.

THE GOOD NEWS
OF JESUS CHRIST

CHAPTER 9

Great and wonderful are your works,
Lord God almighty.

Revelation 15:3

WHAT difference does Jesus' resurrection from the dead make in people's lives? Is it really that important in your life?

The Paschal Mystery

If Jesus had not risen from the dead, we might never have heard of him, and Christianity would not exist. Jesus' life would have been a failure and would have ended in defeat. There would not be much good news to share, and no one would have wanted to write a New Testament.

But Jesus did rise from the dead. The testimony of his followers and of believers from the beginning has been absolutely clear. Soon after his death on the cross and his burial, they began to experience his presence in a whole new way. The gospels do not describe his resurrection but speak of finding the empty tomb. According to Paul's account in 1 Corinthians 15:3–8, Jesus appeared to more than five hundred of his disciples.

Was it easy for all the followers of Jesus to believe that he had risen? Eyewitness accounts in the gospels relate that it was difficult for some. When the apostle Thomas, for example, heard the testimony of others to the resurrection, he did not believe it at first. When he heard that others had seen the Lord, Thomas said, "Unless I see the mark of the nails in his hands and put my finger into the nailmarks and put my hand into his side, I will not believe." Then a week later, when the risen Christ appeared to the disciples, he said to Thomas, "Put your finger here and see my hands, and bring your hand and put it into my side, and do not be unbelieving, but believe." Thomas's response was "My Lord and my God!" (John 20:25, 27–28). It took a lot to get Thomas to believe!

The resurrection of Jesus was a unique event, of course. Nothing like it had ever happened before. It astonished the followers of Jesus and challenged everything that they knew. In the resurrection of Jesus, God had brought to completion the salvation of the world and all that he wanted to accomplish in Christ. Jesus' crucifixion was not his final moment. It was in the resurrection that he was victorious over sin and death.

After a short time the appearances of the risen Christ came to an end, for Christ had to return to his Father. We call Christ's return to the Father his *ascension*. Jesus, risen from the dead, had entered into a whole new life, one that could not be limited to an earthly existence. That is why the gospel writer said that Jesus "parted from them and was taken up to heaven" (Luke 24:51).

With the ascension Jesus Christ was exalted in glory and enthroned at the right hand of the Father (Acts 2:33–35). There Jesus is our high priest, the one mediator between God and humanity (1 Timothy 2:5). This means that Jesus Christ offers all our prayers to the Father. This is why we pray at Mass, "Through him, with him, in him, in the unity of the Holy Spirit, all glory and honor is yours, almighty Father, for ever and ever. Amen."

For us the resurrection and ascension of Christ are not simply distant memories. We share in the new life of Christ right now. Just as we were once dead in sin, now we rise with Christ in Baptism to newness of life. This is our sharing in the death and resurrection of Jesus Christ, our paschal lamb, and the salvation he won for us.

Some people have spent a lifetime trying to summarize the wondrous events of Jesus' life, his teaching, and all that he did for us out of love. But we can summarize it all in one simple phrase: the paschal mystery. The *paschal mystery* refers to the passion, death, resurrection, and ascension of Christ. These are the most important events in our redemption. Through these events Jesus Christ brought salvation to the whole world.

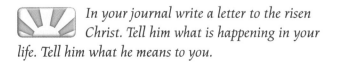 *In your journal write a letter to the risen Christ. Tell him what is happening in your life. Tell him what he means to you.*

The Truth of the Gospels

Because of the resurrection Christians see the world in a whole new way. Just as a lamp lights up a dark room, so our belief in the resurrection enables us to see Jesus more clearly and to understand his message. This was the experience of Jesus' first followers and of the early Church community. That is why the gospels and the rest of the New Testament were written: to celebrate the paschal mystery and to share the good news of Christ in the light of the resurrection.

Some people, however, may have doubts about the truth of the gospels. They feel that the New Testament accounts are incredible, that they cannot be believed or trusted. They wonder how Jesus could have done the things that he did.

How can we be sure that the gospel picture of Jesus is really true? What would you say?

Even for nonbelievers there are certain things about the New Testament that cannot be denied. The first has to do with the closest followers of Jesus, the twelve apostles. As fishermen they had to be strong, rough, and ready. They were full of life and knew what hard work was. It would have been unlikely for such no-nonsense individuals to have been fooled easily. Only someone powerful in word and deed could have attracted the apostles, convincing them to follow him and give up everything.

Jesus was just that type of individual. When he asked the apostles to follow him, they left everything and went everywhere with him. However, when Jesus was condemned to death by crucifixion, the apostles were afraid that they would suffer the same fate. All but one deserted Jesus for fear of their lives. They went and hid.

Only one thing transformed this fearful band: the resurrection. When they recognized the risen Lord and knew that he was still among them, they were filled with excitement. Transformed by the power of the Holy Spirit, they went out and boldly proclaimed the good news of Jesus. They did this with a unanimous voice. Remember that these were simple fishermen, not educated or used to public speaking. How could they have changed so quickly if the risen Christ were not with them?

Moreover the message that they shared was an unpopular one. Suddenly, after the resurrection, they as Jews were preaching a message that all Jews would find blasphemous: that a man should be worshiped as God. Their message was one that the rest of the world would say made no sense. Would anyone want to believe in a savior who had to die? Was it sensible to believe that a small-town carpenter from the middle of nowhere was now Lord of the universe? Yet this is exactly what the early Church preached.

Scripture UPDATE

Mary Magdalene is the only person to appear in all four gospel accounts as a primary witness to Christ's resurrection. Her testimony was crucial to the early Church. This is an amazing fact when we consider that at the time of Jesus a woman's testimony was not legally acceptable. It was accepted only when verified by the testimony of men. This acceptance of Mary Magdalene is another surprising turn of events in the gospels.

Filled with Surprises

For people of the first century and for us, too, each page of the gospels is filled with surprises. Who would have imagined that the Son of God would appear on earth as a poor, unknown Nazarene, yet filled with love, gentleness, and the best of human qualities? Who would have thought that the Savior of the world would spend his time with sinners and lepers and all the outcasts of society? Who would have thought that the Messiah would criticize those in power and yet find time for those who had no power, especially women and children? No one could have thought up a religious leader like Jesus, least of all the apostles.

Not only that, but the first followers of Jesus were hated for their message. The early Church was even outlawed in the Roman Empire. At first it had to be an underground Church willing to suffer persecution and martyrdom. Belief in Jesus could send people to the Roman Coliseum, where they would be fed to lions.

The early Christians gained nothing of material importance because of their faith in the risen Christ. They did not become wealthy or powerful. Saint Paul said, "I even consider everything as a loss because of the supreme good of knowing Christ Jesus my Lord. For his sake I have accepted the loss of all things and I consider them so much rubbish, that I may gain Christ and be found in him" (Philippians 3:8–9). No one could say these words without being sure of the truth. People have trusted in the truth of the New Testament for almost two thousand years. It is the truth that we, too, can experience in the risen Christ.

The Providence of God

Knowing that Jesus had risen from the dead changed the apostles forever. The risen Christ was with them. Now they were certain that everything Jesus had taught them was true.

At the heart of Jesus' teaching was his concern for his Father and the fulfillment of the Father's will. Jesus' entire life centered on his Father. He wanted his disciples to know that God is personally concerned for each one of us. God loves us so much, in fact, that he sent his Son to redeem us. Jesus' first recorded words in Luke's Gospel tell us of his mission: He had to be about his Father's work (Luke 2:49).

Jesus used every moment to make his Father known. If a few sparrows settled near the place where Jesus was speaking, they could be used as an example in his teaching. One day he said, "Are not five sparrows sold for two small coins? Yet not one of them has escaped the notice of God. Even the hairs of your head have all been counted. Do not be afraid. You are worth more than many sparrows" (Luke 12:6–7). How wonderful to know that God cares for each one of us so much!

We use a special term to help us remember this overwhelming love and care of God; it is God's providence. *God's providence* is his personal concern for each of his creatures. And this was Jesus' message: Trust God because God cares. Jesus tells everyone of every age about the providence of God. "Do not worry and say, 'What are we to eat?' or 'What are we to drink?' or 'What are we to wear?' All these things the pagans seek. Your heavenly Father knows that you need them all" (Matthew 6:31–32).

CATHOLIC ID

Many Catholic homes display a crucifix, a symbol of God's providence in sending us his Son as our redeemer. Do you know what the letters INRI stand for on the crucifix? According to John's Gospel an inscription was placed on the cross that read in Latin *Iesus Nazarenus Rex Iudaeorum* (meaning "Jesus of Nazareth, King of the Jews"). So the INRI on a crucifix is made up of the first letter of each word in the Latin inscription.

Providence and Prayer

Does the providence of God mean that we get anything we want at any time we want it? Does it mean that God will answer every prayer exactly the way we want? It may be that what we ask for is not good for us. For example, we might ask God to help us pass every test we take with flying colors but without studying. This would be a foolish thing to ask, since it would hurt us in our future lives. God would never want to do that.

When we place our trust in God's providence, we know that everything will work out for the best. Each of our prayers, no matter how brief, receives God's personal and undivided attention. The answer to every prayer is yes—from God's point of view. But God may not answer us exactly as we expect. And this may be hard for us to understand. When we see God face to face, we will know all the reasons for God's providence.

Sons and Daughters of God

In Jesus' teaching on the Father, there is something for everyone. For a young person who feels unloved or abandoned, Jesus has a special message: The Father cares. Our heavenly Father makes the "sun rise on the bad and the good, and causes rain to fall on the just and the unjust" (Matthew 5:45). No one is forgotten by God; no one is ever abandoned for a single instant. God's offer of forgiveness extends always to each and every one of his children. This is why Jesus could tell the story of the prodigal son (Luke 15:11–32).

In his Father's plan, Jesus tells us, there is a special place for each one of us. It is like having our own room at home where things are familiar, warm, and secure. "In my Father's house there are many dwelling places. If there were not, would I have told you that I am going to prepare a place for you? And if I go and prepare a place for you, I will come back again and take you to myself, so that where I am you also may be" (John 14:2–3).

Sometimes a person may ask, "How does God see me? Am I just one of the crowd?" It is the individual person whom God loves. Because we are one with Christ, we are truly sons and daughters of this one Father of all. That is why we can pray both individually and as a community the words Jesus taught us.

 Close your eyes and quietly pray the Our Father.

The Kingdom of God

The idea of God's providence can also be seen in Jesus' teaching about the kingdom of God. According to the Gospel of Mark, Jesus opened his public ministry by proclaiming, "The kingdom of God is at hand. Repent, and believe in the gospel" (Mark 1:15). What did Jesus mean by the phrase *kingdom of God*? He used it often in his preaching and teaching but never defined it.

To understand what that sense was, we turn to the Old Testament. There we find that God is frequently referred to as king. Why did the Old Testament writers choose this word? The king was supposed to be like the father of his nation. He was to care for his people, protect them from danger, and guarantee justice, especially for the weak and oppressed. God was, therefore, their king because he took care of them.

Jesus and the people of his time were familiar with this idea of God as a king. To be part of God's kingdom meant to be loved and protected by God. The *kingdom of God* was a symbol reminding everyone that God was the Lord of the universe, who would take care of his people and bring them salvation. Members of God's kingdom would return God's love and follow God's law. God would have a central place in their lives.

The kingdom of God was not a place; it was God's rule and reign over people's lives. Jesus wanted everyone to know that they would find the kingdom of God in him. Pointing to himself he said, "Behold, the kingdom of God is among you" (Luke 17:21). Jesus was saying that the kingdom had already burst upon the world in a marvelous way through his teaching, miracles, and healing ministry. God's kingdom is found in Jesus. What a wonderful way for God to care for his people and bring us salvation.

Jesus also taught that the kingdom of God was not yet complete. It had come in a dramatic way with Jesus, but as he said, it is like a seed that was planted (Matthew 13:18–23, 31–32). The kingdom still needs to grow and be nourished by us, Jesus' disciples. We must, therefore, look to the future as we celebrate and proclaim God's saving activity in the world. We are to take an active part in making that kingdom grow, a kingdom of justice and love. That is why we pray "thy kingdom come."

Jesus was so excited about the kingdom of God that he wanted all people to know about it. So he gathered around himself a community of disciples, the Church. He did this so that we could proclaim the good news of the kingdom and work for its completion. The Church and the kingdom of God are closely connected. Catholics believe that the Church is "on earth the seed and the beginning of that kingdom" (*Catechism*, 541).

CATHOLIC TEACHINGS

About the Kingdom

All of us must work for the coming of God's kingdom, as we pray in the Lord's Prayer. To enter God's kingdom the Church teaches that we must turn toward God and do his will. And we remember that it is God's kingdom, not ours. The final completion of the kingdom will happen as God wants.

You may wish to make a collage that will help others understand the meaning of God's kingdom. Use magazine pictures or your own original art to show what happens when God is at the center of our lives.

Life in Christ

If we want to know God, we look to Jesus. If we want to know what God asks of us, we listen to the message of Jesus. Only the risen Christ, living with us forever, can lead us to the love of God our Father. Jesus Christ is our teacher, and as he himself said, "My teaching is not my own but is from the one who sent me" (John 7:16).

On the night before he died, Jesus stressed three very important truths. He wanted to emphasize to the apostles the necessity of being united with him. These truths are:

• Only by a life united to Jesus will we ever reach the Father's house—heaven, our true home. Jesus said, "No one comes to the Father except through me" (John 14:6).

• Not only are we to be aware of our life in union with Christ, but we are also required to live it in a practical way. This we do by loving action and service on behalf of others every day. Jesus said, "This is my commandment: love one another as I love you" (John 15:12).

• Because we are united to Jesus in faith and Baptism, our lives are Christ-filled. Jesus said, "I am in my Father and you are in me and I in you" (John 14:20).

Getting to know Jesus is the work of a lifetime. We have only "scratched the surface." But that is all right. Jesus is patient. After all, he said to us, "I am with you always, until the end of the age" (Matthew 28:20).

things to think about

Why do you think getting to know Jesus is the work of a lifetime?

Someone once said that there is a little bit of the apostle Thomas in each of us. How do you react to that statement?

WORDS TO REMEMBER

Find and define the following:

God's providence _____

_____

_____

paschal mystery_____

_____

_____

things to share

If you were going to explain to someone the phrase "thy kingdom come" in the Lord's Prayer, how would you go about it?

One day a friend comes to you and says, "Why should I pray? After all, to God I'm just one person among millions of others." Basing your response on the teaching of Jesus, what would you say to your friend?

OnLine WITH THE PARISH

One simple way to work for God's kingdom is to encourage those who have more to share with those who have less. It has been said that the coat hanging unused in your closet belongs to the one who needs it. Meet with other parish groups, and help to plan a clothing drive for those in need. Plan on ways you will assist in collecting, sorting, and delivering the clothes to local Church or civic agencies.

Why can we say that the gospel message is believable? Name one reason that convinces you.

1

Was it easy for all the followers of Jesus to believe that he had risen from the dead? Explain.

2

Does the providence of God mean that we can get anything we want at any time we want it?

3

What did Jesus mean when he spoke of the kingdom of God?

4

What did Jesus mean when he said, "No one comes to the Father except through me"?

5

Life in the Spirit

Jesus said, "Whoever does not take up his cross and follow after me is not worthy of me" (Matthew 10:38). What a tall order! How can we ever hope to follow in Jesus' footsteps? How can we ever hope to carry a cross in life? Only if we rely on God's care for us. Jesus told us, "Everything is possible to one who has faith" (Mark 9:23). What crosses do you bear in your life? Ask Jesus to help you bear them with love as he did.

CHAPTER 10

THE LORD AND GIVER OF LIFE

Come, Holy Spirit,
fill the hearts of your faithful.

WHAT do you think of when you hear the word spirit? What image comes into your mind? Does this image have anything to do with your understanding of the Holy Spirit?

Holy Spirit window, St. Peter's Basilica, Rome

Third Person of the Trinity

Sometimes called the forgotten Person of the Blessed Trinity, the Holy Spirit is the Lord and Giver of Life. Why "forgotten"? Why "Lord"? Why "Giver of Life"?

Forgotten   When you think of God, how often do you think about the Holy Spirit? Perhaps not very often. Most people probably think about God the Father or God the Son when they think of God. Even in the celebration of the liturgy, we tend to think of our prayers as addressed to God the Father through Jesus Christ our Lord. But when we do this, we forget that there is another part to the prayers of the Church: We always pray to the Father, through the Son, in the Holy Spirit.

The Holy Spirit, the third Person of the Blessed Trinity, may also be forgotten for a simple reason. It may be easier for human beings to see the Father and the Son as divine Persons. Even traditional artworks may have contributed to the problem. How many times have we seen the Holy Spirit pictured as a dove? The dove is a wonderful symbol for the Holy Spirit, of course, because it comes from the Bible itself. Nevertheless it may make it harder for some to relate to the Holy Spirit as a divine Person.

Lord   One of the titles for God with which we are most familiar is "Lord." Just think how often the title is used in the Old Testament. Rather than referring to God as *Yahweh*, the sacred name of God that was given to Moses, the Old Testament writers often used *Lord*. This was done out of reverence for God's name.

Christians know the Lord God of the Old Testament as God the Father. And because Jesus is the only Son of God, he, too, is Lord. But do Catholics usually think of the Holy Spirit as the Lord? Perhaps not often enough. Remember, the Persons of the Blessed Trinity are distinct but equal. If the Father and the Son are both Lord, the Holy Spirit must be Lord, too. *Lord* is a title that refers to divinity. Each time we recite the Nicene Creed, we recall that the Holy Spirit "is worshiped and glorified" with the Father and the Son.

Giver of Life   The Holy Spirit is the only Person of the Blessed Trinity who is called the Giver of Life. This is true for a number of reasons. Probably the most important reason is that the Holy Spirit dwells in us through sanctifying grace. This means that we share in the divine life through the power of the Holy Spirit. Saint Paul explained this truth another way. In 1 Corinthians 6:19, he reminded the early Christians that they were temples of the Holy Spirit.

There is something else important to think about. Did you know that you cannot have faith unless the Holy Spirit gives it to you? We do not usually think of faith in this way, but this is one more reason why we call the Holy Spirit the Giver of Life. The Church teaches that without the Holy Spirit we cannot have faith, we cannot believe. This Catholic truth is stated dramatically in the New Testament. There we read, "No one can say, 'Jesus is Lord,' except by the holy Spirit" (1 Corinthians 12:3).

What does this mean for our lives? Actually a great deal. Our life of faith comes to us from the Holy Spirit. The Holy Spirit, therefore, is closer to us and more important to us than most of us realize. The Holy Spirit is the Lord and Giver of Life. Knowing all this, will you think differently about the Holy Spirit from now on? Are you ready to learn even more? Don't let the Holy Spirit remain the forgotten Person of the Blessed Trinity for you.

 Pray the prayer to the Holy Spirit found at the beginning of this chapter.

The Holy Spirit in Scripture

Have you ever heard anyone say, "Where there is life, there is breath"? Consider the simple act of taking a deep breath. At that moment our lungs are filled with life-giving oxygen. Without breathing, we would not stay alive very long. Breath is essential to life.

The biblical writers thought about the life of the world in much the same way. They said that the "breath," or Spirit, of Yahweh was present at creation and kept it in existence. The world would be lifeless without this Spirit of God. That is why the phrase *Spirit of Yahweh* is found frequently in the Old Testament.

What did the word *spirit* mean for the biblical writers? It had a variety of meanings: breath, wind, life, soul, mind, and power. At the beginning of the Old Testament, God's work is described as a wind that "swept over the waters" at creation (Genesis 1:2) and as "the breath of life" giving life to Adam (Genesis 2:7). God is seen as acting through his Spirit.

Later in the Old Testament, the Spirit of Yahweh gave the early leaders of Israel great power and strength. In helping to form God's people, they were able to do marvelous deeds only because God's Spirit was with them. Think about Samson, who rescued God's people from their Philistine enemies. One account about this legendary strongman explained the reason for his strength. As the story goes, one day Samson was attacked by a roaring lion. "But the spirit of the LORD came upon Samson, and although he had no weapons, he tore the lion in pieces" (Judges 14:6).

Finish this sentence: The breath of the Spirit is like . . . .

Christians know these words of Joel very well, for they appear again in the second chapter of the Acts of the Apostles. The apostle Peter quoted these words on the day of Pentecost. He tried to explain that the time of the Messiah had come, that God's work had now been brought to completion in Jesus Christ. Peter and the other disciples received the Holy Spirit because they were the followers of the risen Christ. Led by the Spirit, they would now share in Jesus' work on earth.

Alive in the Spirit

In one of the best-known passages of the Bible, the prophet Ezekiel writes about an unusual vision he had. In the vision the Spirit of Yahweh leads Ezekiel to the center of a plain filled with dried human bones. Suddenly the bones begin to rattle as they come together. After they are covered with flesh, the Spirit of God enters into them. Then they come alive and stand. By sharing this vision of the bones, Ezekiel is saying that the Spirit of Yahweh gives life—and can even give life to the dead (Ezekiel 37:1–14).

 You may wish to read this famous passage in Ezekiel.

Another passage in the Bible, this one from the prophet Joel in the Old Testament, helps us to discover more about the Spirit of God for our own day. Joel speaks about the future and the time of the promised Messiah. Here the Spirit of God is described as God's gift to those who act on his behalf. In this famous passage God is saying,

> Then afterward I will pour out
>   my spirit upon all mankind.
> Your sons and daughters shall prophesy,
>   your old men shall dream dreams,
>   your young men shall see visions.
> Then everyone shall be rescued
>   who calls on the name of the LORD.
> Joel 3:1, 5

In every age God's Spirit is given to those who share in God's work.

Scripture UPDATE

Saint Paul used a rich image to describe Christians. In 1 Corinthians 6:19 he called each one of us a "temple" of the Holy Spirit. When he wrote this, Paul was thinking about the Temple of Jerusalem and how important it was in Jewish life.

Before the Temple was even built, the ark of the covenant, the symbol of God's presence with his people, was placed in a tent. A tent was used because the Israelites were nomads, wandering from place to place. Finally, after they had settled in the promised land, they constructed a permanent dwelling for the ark. This was the magnificent Temple of Jerusalem. There the ark of the covenant was placed in the holy of holies, the very heart of the Temple. This place was so sacred that the high priest alone could enter it.

The Temple was revered by all the people as the place where God dwelled among them in a special way. Knowing this, we can see what Saint Paul had in mind when he said that we are temples of the Holy Spirit. God's dwelling place is no longer to be regarded as being in one building. Now the Holy Spirit dwells in each of us. Can you imagine what the world would be like if all the followers of Jesus were to understand and appreciate what this means for their lives? It would change the world overnight!

117

The Holy Spirit in Christ's Life

Modern Catholics may be surprised to find out how closely involved the Holy Spirit was in the life of Jesus. From the very beginning it was the Holy Spirit who came upon the Blessed Virgin Mary before Jesus' birth (Luke 1:35). Each time we recite the Nicene Creed, we profess our belief that at the incarnation the Son of God was born of the Virgin Mary "by the power of the Holy Spirit."

Later when John the Baptist baptized Jesus at the Jordan River, the Holy Spirit was present again. A dove was the sign of the Holy Spirit's presence. After Jesus' baptism the Holy Spirit drew him into the desert; there Jesus overcame the temptations of Satan. Then Jesus began his public life "in the power of the Spirit" (Luke 4:14). On returning to Nazareth, his hometown, Jesus announced the fulfillment of Isaiah's prophecy. Jesus said:

> "The Spirit of the Lord is upon me,
> because he has anointed me
>   to bring glad tidings to the poor.
> He has sent me to proclaim liberty to captives
>   and recovery of sight to the blind,
>   to let the oppressed go free,
> and to proclaim a year acceptable to the Lord."
> Luke 4:18–19

On the night before he died, Jesus promised his apostles that a new Helper would come to them. Jesus told them, "I will ask the Father, and he will give you another Advocate to be with you always, the Spirit of truth" (John 14:16–17).

To understand what Jesus is saying to us, we must know the meaning of the word *advocate*. In the New Testament the word *advocate*, or *paraclete*, has many meanings. It certainly can mean helper, but it means much more. An advocate is someone who speaks for others, who defends others and pleads for them. An advocate is also a comforter, a consoler, an intercessor, and a teacher. The Holy Spirit, then, is our intercessor, consoler, and teacher. He is the Advocate promised by the risen Lord to be with and for his disciples.

The coming of the Holy Spirit was described in John's Gospel as taking place on Easter. After Jesus' death and resurrection, his apostles were afraid that they, too, would be killed. So they hid behind locked doors. John explains what happened next:

> Jesus came and stood in their midst and said to them, "Peace be with you." When he had said this, he showed them his hands and his side. The disciples rejoiced when they saw the Lord. Jesus said to them again, "Peace be with you. As the Father has sent me, so I send you." And when he had said this, he breathed on them and said to them, "Receive the holy Spirit."
> John 20:19–22

CATHOLIC TEACHINGS

About the Holy Spirit

How do we know the Holy Spirit, and how do we keep the Holy Spirit central in our lives? The *Catechism* (688) lists different ways. These include:

- Sacred Scripture, which was inspired by the Holy Spirit
- the tradition of the Church
- the teaching authority of the Church, which the Holy Spirit guides
- the sacraments and liturgy of the Church, in which we pray and worship together through the power of the Holy Spirit, who sanctifies us
- all our prayers, in which the Holy Spirit intercedes for us
- the lives of the saints and the ministries of the Church, in which the Holy Spirit brings us his holiness

Pentecost

Luke's account in the Acts of the Apostles describes the coming of the Holy Spirit in a different way, a description more familiar to most people. In Acts the Holy Spirit comes upon the community of Christians in Jerusalem on the Jewish harvest feast of Pentecost (Acts 2:1–11). It was the fiftieth day after Passover, a time for the Jews to rejoice at the rich blessings God had bestowed upon Israel.

With the coming of the Holy Spirit, Pentecost would now take on new meaning for Christians. Luke said that "suddenly there came from the sky a noise like a strong driving wind." Then he said that "tongues as of fire" came to rest on each of the disciples. "They were all filled with the holy Spirit" (Acts 2:2–4).

For the first Christians this day of Pentecost was the occasion for Jesus to pour out the Holy Spirit upon them, giving them an abundance of the gifts of the Spirit. The risen Christ was sharing his life with them—and with us—in the power of the Holy Spirit. Pentecost, therefore, was the completion of Christ's passover. The coming of the Holy Spirit is the completion of the paschal mystery—all that Jesus Christ did for us.

Have there been times in your life when you have felt the power of the Holy Spirit? Tell about them.

One of the most recognizable stained-glass windows in the world is the window behind the main altar in Saint Peter's Basilica in the Vatican. In the window the Holy Spirit is symbolized as a dove. It reminds us of Jesus' baptism by John at the Jordan. Perhaps even more than this, it reminds us that at Baptism we are made a new creation through the power of the Holy Spirit. The biblical symbol of a dove goes all the way back to the Book of Genesis. In the story of the flood, Noah releases a dove to see whether or not the land has been renewed (Genesis 8:8–12). Thus the dove became a symbol of new life, of a new creation.

Guided by the Spirit

Filled with the Holy Spirit, the early Christians went out with great excitement to bring Christ to others. These once-frightened disciples were given great power, courage, strength, and authority by the Holy Spirit. Jesus had told them, "You will receive power when the holy Spirit comes upon you, and you will be my witnesses in Jerusalem, throughout Judea and Samaria, and to the ends of the earth" (Acts 1:8).

Although the apostles had spent some of the best days of their lives with Jesus, they did not know him as fully as they thought. Jesus himself understood this. That is why Jesus said to them, "I have much more to tell you, but you cannot bear it now. But when he comes, the Spirit of truth, he will guide you to all truth" (John 16:12–13).

The coming of the Holy Spirit made a big difference in the lives of the apostles. Because Jesus sent the Holy Spirit to them, they were now ready to grasp all that he wanted them to know. Recall Jesus' words to the apostles, "The Advocate, the holy Spirit that the Father will send in my name—he will teach you everything and remind you of all that I told you" (John 14:26).

With memories refreshed and enlivened by the Holy Spirit, the apostles were able to give witness to the Jesus that they knew. The man they knew and with whom they walked was the Lord Jesus Christ, the God-Man—not dead, but alive! The Holy Spirit's coming enabled the apostles to recall and present the teachings that Jesus handed over to them for the Church throughout the ages. They now knew and understood their mission.

Today the Holy Spirit is still guiding Jesus' disciples. It is the Holy Spirit who guides the missionary activity of the Church. It is the Holy Spirit who draws so many people to the Church. It is the Holy Spirit who strengthens members of the Church to speak out against oppression, injustice, and poverty in our world.

Are you ever aware of the Holy Spirit working in the life of the Church? Give one example.

The Life of Grace

We are temples of the Holy Spirit. Through Baptism we have been initiated into the life of sanctifying grace, a participation in the very life of God.

Our experience of the Holy Spirit, the sanctifier, does not end with sanctifying grace, however. The Church teaches us that the Holy Spirit is active in our lives through actual graces. *Actual graces* are interventions of God in our daily lives. These interventions are urgings or promptings from the Holy Spirit. Like sparks that can ignite a fire, these graces help us to deepen our Christian life and live the good news of Jesus as members of the Church.

There are many examples of actual graces. The Holy Spirit gives them to us either directly or indirectly through other people and events in our lives. These include the good example of others or the awareness to do good that we might gain from reading a book. Actual graces might also include the feelings that come spontaneously into our lives and that help lead us to holiness.

What would happen if the Holy Spirit were no longer present? Only then might we truly understand what he means to us. Like a world without water, we could not really live without the Holy Spirit. We sometimes forget how important water is until we do not have it. Without water, green fields dry up and become deserts. Without the Holy Spirit, our spiritual lives would be much the same; they would wither away and become desertlike. The Church reminds us of this truth when we pray these words:

> When you hide your face, they are lost.
>   When you take away their breath, they perish
>   and return to the dust from which they came.
> When you send forth your breath, they are
>   created,
>   and you renew the face of the earth.
> Psalm 104:29–30

121

things to think about

Name one new idea about the Holy Spirit that you learned this week. Tell why it was new for you and what that means for you today.

After learning so much about the Holy Spirit, do you think that you will pray in the same way as you have in the past? Why or why not?

things to share

Many Catholics are not used to referring to the Holy Spirit as Lord. How would you explain to someone that the Holy Spirit is the Lord and Giver of Life?

Describe what the world might be like if everyone were to realize that through Baptism we become temples of the Holy Spirit.

WORDS TO REMEMBER

Find and define the following:

Holy Spirit _____

_____

_____

actual graces _____

_____

_____

OnLine WITH THE PARISH

The Holy Spirit gives us actual graces to live out our Christian lives together. Very often these actual graces come to us through other people. What example can you offer to your parish family so that you might be an occasion of actual graces for others? Make sure that your example is practical and that it can be accomplished.

What do we mean when we say in the Nicene Creed, "With the Father and the Son he [the Holy Spirit] is worshiped and glorified"?

1

Why do we call the Holy Spirit the Advocate or Paraclete?

2

Why is the Holy Spirit the Giver of Life?

3

Give some examples of actual graces.

4

Explain in your own words what Saint Paul meant when he said, "No one can say, 'Jesus is Lord,' except by the holy Spirit."

5

Life
in the Spirit

The Holy Spirit is calling us to build up the Church and renew the world. We are reminded of this when we pray the ancient words "Send forth your Spirit and they shall be created, and you shall renew the face of the earth."

Use these words as your prayer this week. As you pray, think of the many modern witnesses who are helping to renew the face of the earth: environmentalists, those who work for nonviolence and social justice, and those who work to end racism and sexism in our world. Think, too, of those who work with the poorest of the poor.

CHAPTER 11

THE MYSTERY OF THE CHURCH

You are fellow citizens with the holy ones
and members of the household of God,
built upon the foundation of
the apostles and prophets.

Ephesians 2:19–20

SATURDAY evening a tornado hit with such great fury that it devastated the small town. Even the Catholic church was destroyed. The next morning Mass was celebrated in the public school gym, one of the few buildings left standing. As the people of the parish gathered together, the pastor reminded them that even though their building was gone, they were still the Church.

More Than Meets the Eye

Some people may be surprised at the pastor's words about being the Church. But he was right. The Church is more than buildings. It is really a great mystery, a mystery so deep that it is difficult to describe the Church in just a few words. That is why we are going to spend four chapters exploring its meaning and depth.

The root meaning of the word *church* is "belonging to the Lord." In the Bible it means "a people called together." The Church is the assembly of those chosen by God in Jesus Christ, the assembly of God's people. Being the Church involves not only being the gathered community but also the process of gathering together. The Church, therefore, is not only an established group but also an event: people coming together, especially for the purpose of worshiping God and serving others. The Church is Christ's faithful people, the people of God.

The People of God

The idea of people of God goes back to Old Testament times. Israel became God's people because God chose it to be his own possession. God said, "I will take you as my own people, and you shall have me as your God" (Exodus 6:7). God's choice of this small nation to be his possession rather than other great nations took place solely from God's love. It was a grace.

Jesus, too, gathered a people to himself. The early Christian community was the new assembly of God's people. After the Pentecost experience in Jerusalem, the community gradually grew through the preaching of the apostles and their helpers. Wherever the people of God were found, they gathered together to hear God's word and to offer eucharistic worship for all that he had done for them.

Just as the choosing of Israel was the result of God's love, so, too, the Church came into being because of the love and grace of God. In fact the early Church

taught that even before the creation of the world, God chose us in Christ (Ephesians 1:4) to be "a chosen race, a royal priesthood, a holy nation, a people of his own" (1 Peter 2:9). We are a people because God dwells in us and moves among us. This means that we are a sign of God's presence in the world. God has chosen his people, and this is a mystery of divine grace.

There is also something more that we should recognize. Using the image of God's people, the writers of the New Testament saw the Church as part of the continuing story of God's dealings with his chosen people. By using the term *people of God*, they were pointing out the bond that existed between the Christian community and the people of Israel.

All this means that the early Christians did not date or place the beginning of God's people from Jesus' birth or ministry. Rather, they looked to the times of Abraham and Moses. That is why among those names that belong to God's people and were adopted by the Church, one of the most meaningful was the name *Israel*. Paul himself addressed the Christian community this way when he wrote, "Peace and mercy be . . . to the Israel of God" (Galatians 6:16).

Jesus once said, "When I am lifted up from the earth, I will draw everyone to myself" (John 12:32). He still works to draw everyone to himself through his people. Just as God once chose and gathered his people by delivering them from Egypt, now he gathers his community, the Church, through the redeeming blood of his Son. Jesus has given himself for us in order to redeem us, "to cleanse for himself a people as his own" (Titus 2:14).

If you were going to describe the Church, how would you go about it? What image would you use? Be original.

127

The Body of Christ

The Church is people, no one of whom is perfect. Paul himself knew this when he worked with the early Christians. When we read his letters in the New Testament, we can see that he ran into many difficulties. There were disagreements among the members of the Church. Some even formed into rival groups, claiming as their authority Peter, Paul, or one of the other leaders of the Church.

Disagreements, of course, are not unusual. They go on in the Church in every age. The Church is a visible organization; and in its human reality, it is often too human. Its human weaknesses offend many and, at times, turn them away. But is the Church only a human organization?

No. The Spirit of the living God is present in the Church. The Church is founded on Jesus Christ and guided by the Holy Spirit. This is why Paul frequently mentioned that Christians are united to Christ in one common life. He taught that the Church is the body of Christ, with the life-giving Holy Spirit flowing through that body. "For in one Spirit we were all baptized into one body, whether Jews or Greeks, slaves or free persons, and we were all given to drink of one Spirit" (1 Corinthians 12:13).

Paul gave us this understanding of the Church as the body of Christ. The experience of his own conversion gave him that wise insight. One day he was on his way to the city of Damascus with one purpose in mind: to destroy the followers of Jesus. Suddenly Christ appeared to him. Paul heard a voice saying to him, "Why are you persecuting me?" When Paul asked who it was he was persecuting, the voice replied, "I am Jesus, whom you are persecuting" (Acts 9:4–5).

Paul got the message! During the rest of his lifetime, he saw more and more the connection between Jesus and his followers. Jesus Christ lives in us and we in him. Paul taught that we are one body; that is, we belong to Christ's body. Each Christian has a special role to play. Each is uniquely related to Christ. "As a body is one though it has many parts, and all the parts of the body, though many, are one body, so also Christ" (1 Corinthians 12:12).

A Unique Image

The individual parts of a human body share a common life and cannot live apart from one another. In the same way we share the life of Christ, the head of the body that is his Church. "Now you are Christ's body, and individually parts of it" (1 Corinthians 12:27). Individually and together we are the fullness of Christ, the whole Christ. If others want to meet Christ now in our time, they meet him in us! What a wonderful way to think of Jesus Christ and his Church.

Paul was not alone in his thinking. His image of the Church as the body of Christ is similar to other New Testament images, such as the image of the vine and branches (John 15:1–8). These comparisons try to express the close connection between Jesus Christ and his people. They also bring out the closeness that Church members must have with one another. After all, we are members of the same body. The Church in the New Testament, then, is most appropriately called the body of Christ. But the image does not replace that of the people of God—it deepens it. The Church is the people of God as the body of Christ.

It is clear, then, that *body of Christ* is a unique image. It expresses a relation between Christ and the Church that is as close as can be imagined. It reminds us that Christ and the Church are so close that no one can come to Christ without the Church. Our personal union with Christ, therefore, also involves our belonging to the Church. This means that no one can be an isolated follower of Jesus Christ; one must be a member of the Church.

The accompanying chart lists some familiar images of the Church. Study them and discuss their meaning for your life.

Other New Testament Images of the Church

Image	Biblical Source	Meaning
ark of salvation	1 Peter 3:19–22	The Church is compared to Noah's ark. As a means of salvation through water, the ark reminds us of Baptism and our initiation into the Church.
bride of Christ	1 Corinthians 11:2	The union of Christ and his members is one of intimate, mutual, and permanent interdependence.
building on a rock	Matthew 16:18–19	*Rock* is a title of God in the Old Testament. The Church teaches and guides us with God's authority.
mother	Revelation 12:17	Through the sacraments the Church brings us into and nourishes us in the divine life.

Scripture UPDATE

In the New Testament and in Catholic writings, the term *body of Christ* is used in three different ways. It can refer to:

- the human body of the historical Jesus
- the sacramental presence of Christ in the Eucharist
- the Church.

Whenever the members of the Church worship together, they are more than an ordinary group of people; they are a people intimately united with their Lord (1 Corinthians 11:27). When they have sinned and they repent, mere human words spoken by a priest become the bearers of divine forgiveness (John 20:23).

We can say that the Church combines what is human and divine, what is earthly and heavenly, and what is found in time and in eternity. Like the moon reflecting the light of the sun, the Church brings the light of Christ to the world. It is clear, then, that the Church is a mystery, a truth of faith that we know only because God revealed it to us.

The Family of God

The Church is a mystery and the union of what is human and divine. We probably do not think of it that way each day, but we should. We can also think of the Church as our family, the family of God. This idea goes back to the earliest times when the Church was spoken of as "the household of God," another way of saying God's family (1 Peter 4:17). We enter this family through Baptism, the sacrament by which we become children of God.

It is in the parish, the basic unit of the Church, that most Catholics live out their membership in the family of God. All the members begin to share a common, or family, life through the sacraments of Baptism, Confirmation, and Eucharist. And these sacraments of initiation, as well as the other sacraments, are celebrated in the parish.

The members of the Church, like the members of any family, are all different. Each has his or her own gifts and talents and graces. Each fills a different role. Some are ordained deacons. Others are ordained priests. Still others are ordained bishops, who share the fullness of the priesthood. Bishops, priests, and deacons are called the clergy. The *clergy* are the members of the Church who have received the sacrament of Holy Orders. Most members of the Church, however, are the laity. The *laity* are the baptized members of the Church.

Human and Divine

It is clear that the Church is an organized community unlike any other. As the people of God, it is a union of people guided by the Holy Spirit and under the direction of its leaders. Like any other group of people, it is both shaped by and shapes history. It rejoices in the goodness of its members but suffers from their weaknesses, too.

As the body of Christ, the Church is made up of both human and divine dimensions. It is presided over by human beings, yet they act with the authority they have received from God (Matthew 18:18). When the Church proclaims God's word in human language, it relies, not on human wisdom, but on the power of the Holy Spirit (1 Corinthians 2:13).

This includes everyone who is not in Holy Orders or who is not a vowed *religious*, a member of a religious order or community. No less than the clergy and religious, the laity have an important part in the whole life of the family of God.

Clergy, religious, and laity depend on one another in the parish family and must work as a team. Paul wrote about the different activities of various members of the Church family. He explained that the smooth functioning of the body depends on the cooperation of all its parts. You may wish to read what he has to say about this in 1 Corinthians 12:18–26.

Among laity, religious, and clergy there must be a deep bond. Each works to bring the risen Christ into the world. Each is able to do this in ways that the other cannot. Each is able to do for people what the other cannot do. Together they complete one another in the sense of being united in Christ for the common good of everyone they meet.

From your experience as a member of a parish, complete the accompanying chart by describing the different functions of parish members.

CATHOLIC ID

One way the laity are actively involved in the life of a parish is through the parish council. A *parish council* is a group of parishioners who are elected or appointed to help the pastor in the administration of the parish. The pastor presides over the council, and council members work closely with him. They advise him about the needs of the parish, including parish finances, education, liturgy, and social justice.

Who's Who in the Parish

Name	Your Description
pastor	
other priests	
deacons	
pastoral ministers	
eucharistic ministers	
lectors	
altar servers	
ushers	
director of religious education	
Catholic school principal	
religious sisters	
religious brothers	
catechists	
teachers	
director of music	
members of parish organizations	

Essential Features

What makes you the person you are? Is it the color of your hair or the fact that you wear glasses? Of course not. Things like these are only superficial, only on the surface. Each of us is so much more. Each of us is unique and has a set of unique characteristics. Without your own unique characteristics, you would not be who you are.

The same is true of the Church. The Church also has certain characteristics, or essential features. Without them the Church would not be the Church that Jesus founded. Four essential features of the Church are that it is one, holy, catholic, and apostolic. These characteristics are so important for Catholics that we profess our belief about them each week at Mass. Let's look at them more closely.

Unity: A Gift Never to Be Lost   When we say that the Church is *one*, we are talking about the unity of the Church. And this unity of the Church comes from its source, the Blessed Trinity. This means that God the Father calls us into the one body of Christ, to whom we belong. The Holy Spirit gives life to that body.

From the earliest times this wonderful unity of the Church has been expressed in its one profession of faith handed on to each generation from the time of the apostles. The unity of the Church is also expressed in the celebration of divine worship, especially the sacraments. We are united in one Baptism and gather as one around the table of the Lord in the Eucharist. Through the sacrament of Holy Orders, the Church can trace its unity back to the time of the apostles. Paul described this unity when he wrote, "Because the loaf of bread is one, we, though many, are one body, for we all partake of the one loaf" (1 Corinthians 10:17). We are one in the Lord and constantly striving for greater unity.

A Work of Grace   The Church is *holy* because our sins are forgiven, and we are sanctified, or made holy, by our union with Christ. Through our Baptism in Christ's death and resurrection, we enter into the life of grace, which is God's own life. God alone is holy, and we participate in that holiness through the Church, especially the sacraments.

Christ so loved the Church that he sent us the Holy Spirit. The Holy Spirit fills and guides the Church for all time. The Church teaches us that as members of the Church we are temples of the Holy Spirit. Through Jesus Christ the whole structure of the Church is held together and "grows into a temple sacred in the Lord"; in Christ we also "are being built together into a dwelling place of God in the Spirit" (Ephesians 2:21–22).

As members of the Church, we are also bearers of the fruits of the Holy Spirit: love, joy, peace, patience, kindness, generosity, faithfulness, gentleness, self-control (Galatians 5:22). As baptized members of the Church, we are a holy people and constantly striving for greater holiness.

At Home Around the World   The Church is *catholic* because it is universal and missionary. It is meant for the whole world and has a message for the whole world. The Church can never be narrow or associate itself with only one place or time. Jesus never placed any limits on the Church, where it was to go or thrive. Rather, the Church must gather to itself all who are called by God.

The Church, therefore, is not called catholic because it does missionary work. Rather, the Church engages in missionary activity precisely because it is catholic and has a message for all. That is why Jesus says, "Go, therefore, and make disciples of all nations" (Matthew 28:19). The Church is catholic and must never rest from bringing Christ to the world. The task is not over until the end of time.

CATHOLIC TEACHINGS

About the Church's Essential Features

It is Christ, through the Holy Spirit, who makes the Church one, holy, catholic, and apostolic. And it is Christ who calls the Church "to realize each of these qualities" (*Catechism*, 811).

Missionary priest, Brothers and Sisters of the Cross, Lebanon

The True Foundation The Church is *apostolic* because it was founded on Christ and the apostles. Jesus chose the apostles to lead the early Church in his name. They were sent by Christ himself—by him and by no other—to be his witnesses "to the ends of the earth" (Acts 1:8). Guided by the Holy Spirit, the apostles handed on the teachings of Christ. That is why the Church always looks back to the apostolic foundation of Peter and the other apostles when it looks for the deposit of faith. This apostolic foundation can never be replaced.

Until Christ comes again at the end of time, the Church will continue in the apostolic tradition under the leadership of the pope and bishops, the successors to the apostles. They teach, sanctify, and govern the Church in the name of Christ. The Church is apostolic and must always strive to stay in tune with its true apostolic foundation.

How would you respond to someone who says that the Church is made up of sinful people and therefore cannot be holy?

Pope John Paul II in Ghana, Africa

133

things to think about

Have you ever thought of yourself as "belonging to the Lord"? What does it mean for you to be chosen by God to be part of his people? How do you show it?

Should people give up on the Church when they hear about or meet Church members—clergy, religious, or laity—who are weak or make mistakes? Discuss responses.

things to share

You invite a friend to go to Mass with you one Sunday. Your friend says to you, "I don't need the Church. I follow Christ in my own way, and that is just as good." Your response?

Share your ideas on what it means for the Church to be both human and divine.

WORDS TO REMEMBER

Find and define the following:

clergy _____
_____
_____

religious _____
_____
_____

laity _____
_____
_____

OnLine WITH THE PARISH

No one in a parish can be just a spectator. That goes for the youngest member as well as the oldest. That is because each member is a member of the body of Christ. Using the chart "Who's Who in the Parish," brainstorm creative ways young people can take an active part in the parish as members of the household of God.

Why is the Church called the people of God?

1

What experience led Saint Paul to his understanding of the Church as the body of Christ?

2

Choose your favorite image of the Church and explain it.

3

Name the characteristics, or essential features, of the Church, and explain why they are so necessary.

4

In your own words tell why the Church is a true mystery of faith.

5

Life
in the Spirit

Use the four essential features of the Church as part of your personal prayer today. Say aloud, "The Church is one." Now pause and think of the many ways this is true and the way you are one in Christ with others in the Church. Next say, "The Church is holy." Now think how you share in the very holiness of God through the Church. Do the same with the words *catholic* and *apostolic*. Remember this time of prayer the next time you join your parish community in professing the faith of the Church at Mass.

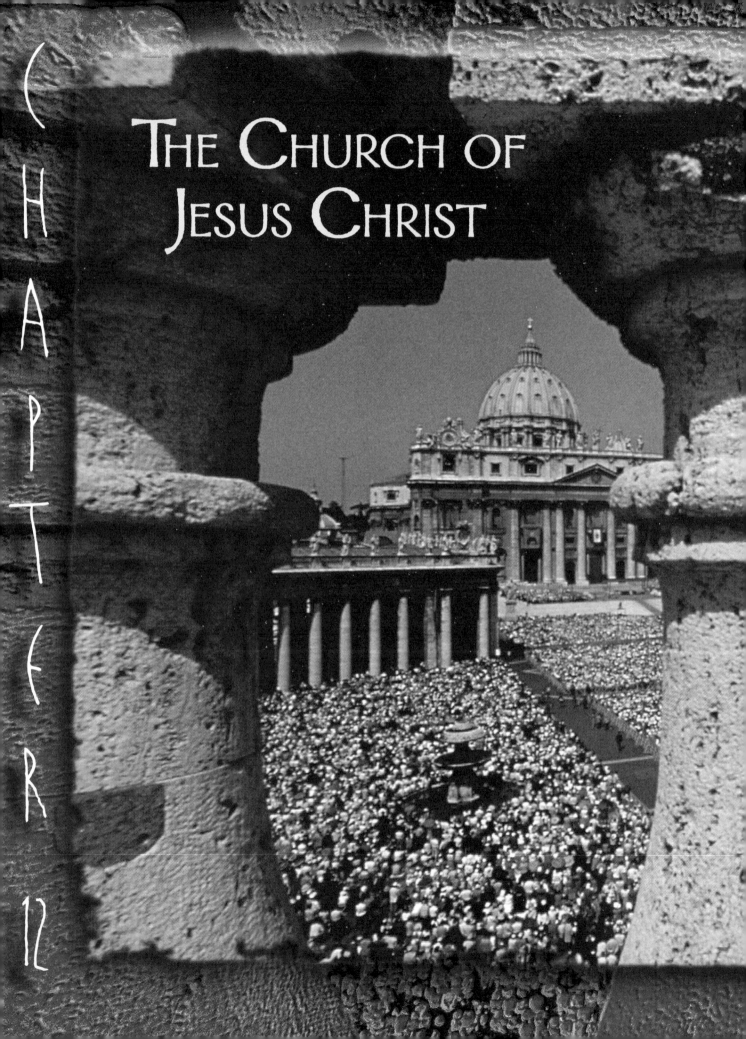

THE CHURCH OF JESUS CHRIST

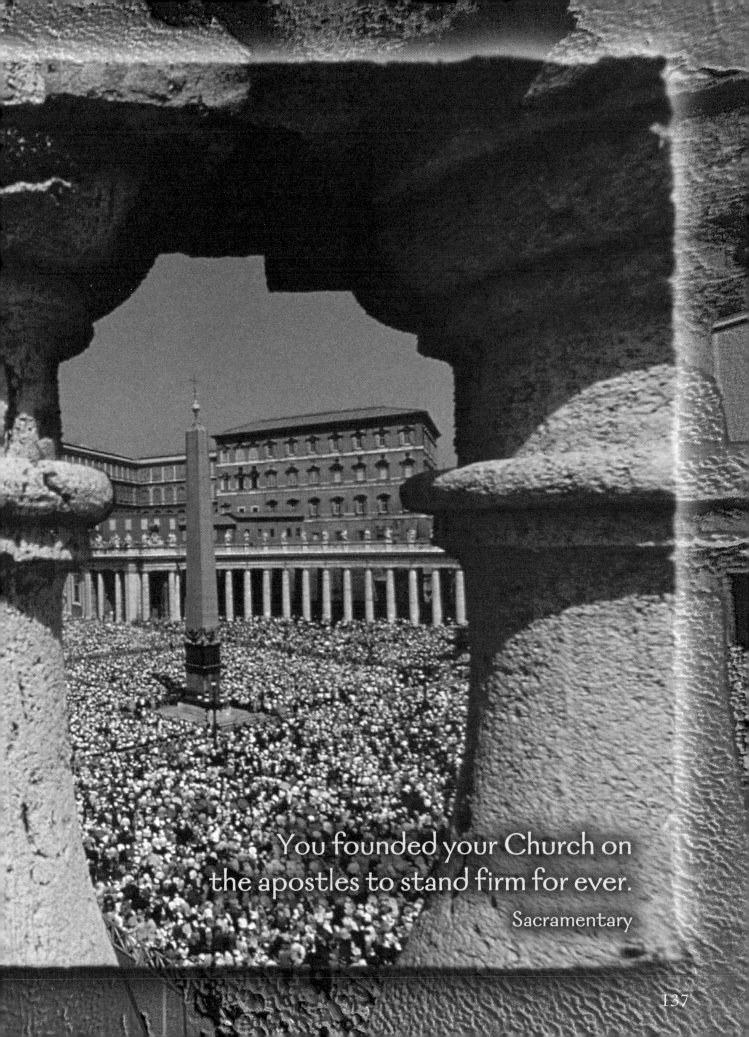

You founded your Church on
the apostles to stand firm for ever.

Sacramentary

If the Church is founded on Christ and the apostles, what happened after the apostles died? Where did the people of God turn for leadership? What do you think?

From Apostle to Bishop

The roots of Church leadership extend back to Jesus and the apostles. Jesus handpicked a group we know as the Twelve and gathered them around himself. These were the apostles. From their close contact with Jesus, they were privileged to know "the mysteries of the kingdom of heaven" (Matthew 13:11). Jesus shared his mission and authority with them. They were to be the pillars upon which he would build his Church.

While Jesus was speaking to the Twelve one day, he asked them what people were saying about him and who he was. It was Simon Peter who finally spoke up and said, "You are the Messiah, the Son of the living God" (Matthew 16:16). Simon was speaking for the other apostles as well when he said that Jesus was the promised Messiah.

Jesus answered this expression of faith in him by changing Simon's name to Peter, meaning "rock." Jesus said, "I say to you, you are Peter, and upon this rock I will build my church, and the gates of the netherworld shall not prevail against it. I will give you the keys to the kingdom of heaven" (Matthew 16:18–19).

Jesus' special recognition of Peter gave him a place of authority above the others but not apart from them. The work of teaching, governing, and sanctifying people in Jesus' name was not to be his alone. It was to be shared by all the apostles with Peter. The Twelve formed a single body, or college; they received their mission together. Although the keys to the kingdom were given to Peter's care, he and the other apostles were the foundation of that Church in which Christ is the cornerstone.

After the ascension of Jesus and Pentecost, the apostles traveled to every part of the world that they knew. With great courage they followed the promptings of the Holy Spirit and established local Churches wherever they went. They did not stay in any one place, however, because they were leaders of the whole Church.

A Wider Ministry   The twelve apostles shared their work with others in the wider ministry of founding and organizing Churches. Sometimes these others, like Paul, were also called "apostles" even though they were not part of the original Twelve. But other names, such as "prophet" and "evangelist," were also used to describe these apostolic leaders. The reason is that official titles had not yet been determined by the Church.

A Local Ministry   Once a local Church became established, the apostolic leaders moved on. But they chose and left behind local Church officers, whom they had ordained by the laying on of hands. These men, too, were called by a number of different titles: "pastor" or "teacher" or "presbyter" (priest, elder) or "bishop" (overseer). The words seemed to have been used interchangeably. Assisted by deacons, these local Church officers presided over their Churches under the authority of the apostles, prophets, and evangelists. But their official titles, like those of the apostolic leaders, had not yet been determined.

The Threefold Ministry   After the Church began to spread around the world, the general traveling ministry of the apostolic leaders became less necessary. It gradually died out as the apostolic leaders passed away. Some of them may have settled in local Churches, as we know James had done in Jerusalem and Timothy in Ephesus. In any event the title of bishop became reserved only for the successors of the apostolic leaders and the title of presbyter (priest) for the other local officers. The title of deacon remained unchanged.

The ministry of the apostles, therefore, was continued and assured in the ministry of the local bishops. These bishops were the vital link to the apostles and thus to Christ himself. By A.D. 110 Ignatius of Antioch could speak of the threefold ministry of bishop, presbyter (priest), and deacon as "established in the farthest parts of the earth." Through the laying on of hands, we have the same threefold ministry today.

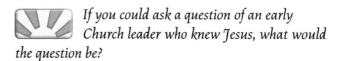 *If you could ask a question of an early Church leader who knew Jesus, what would the question be?*

Acting in the Name of Christ

Imagine that you are a member of the early Church and that it is a time of persecution. During the Eucharist one Sunday, a letter is read to the assembled community. The letter is from the bishop of a neighboring Church. His name is Ignatius, the bishop of Antioch, and not many days ago he was led away in chains. Knowing that you and other Christians might be afraid, Ignatius wants you to be strong in your faith and to know what is important. This is what he writes:

> All of you must follow your bishop, as Jesus followed the Father, and follow the presbyters as you would the apostles; and to the deacons pay respect, as to God's law. Let no one carry on the work of the Church apart from the bishop. There is only one true Eucharist: the one over which the bishop or one of his delegates presides. Wherever the bishop is, that is where the people should be; even as where Jesus is, there is the Universal Church.
> *Letter to the Smyrnaeans, 8*

What a clear picture Ignatius presents of the Church. The people of God are assembled at the altar, with the bishop or one of his presbyters presiding over the celebration of the Eucharist. The bishop stands at the center of the community. Assisted by the presbyters and deacons, he leads the Church with the authority of the apostles and in the name of Jesus. In fact he is the vital link to them in the life of the Church.

How important is the bishop? Very important! Without him there would be no presbyters (priests) or deacons because they are ordained by the bishop. This means that there could be no Eucharist and that most of the other sacraments could not be celebrated. Without the bishop the link to Christ through the apostles would be missing. That is why Cyprian, a third-century Father of the Church, could say, "The bishop is in the Church and the Church in the bishop."

Teaching, Governing, Sanctifying

Jesus wanted all his disciples to be servants of one another, not masters. He said, "Let the greatest among you be as the youngest, and the leader as the servant," and "I am among you as the one who serves" (Luke 22:26, 27). This does not mean, however, that no one was to have authority in the Church. Every human organization must have some authority to help it identify itself, to help bring unity, and to resolve any conflicts or problems. The Church is no different.

Jesus is the source of all authority and ministry in the Church. Knowing how important this authority would be, he shared it with the apostles and those who were to succeed them. That is why bishops succeed the apostles in their office of teaching, governing, and sanctifying in the name of Christ.

Teaching   The bishops are the chief teachers of the Church. As the chief teachers, they succeed to the office of the apostles and prophets. As links to the apostles, the bishops are charged with the sacred duty of passing on the complete and authentic teaching of Jesus and the apostolic Church. Guided by the Holy Spirit, they are to transmit and make clear what has been revealed to us by God; they are entrusted by God to safeguard the great deposit of faith that belongs to the Church. This work of the bishops is done as a service to the other members of the Church so that our faith may rest secure on a strong foundation.

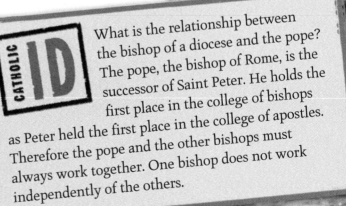

What is the relationship between the bishop of a diocese and the pope? The pope, the bishop of Rome, is the successor of Saint Peter. He holds the first place in the college of bishops as Peter held the first place in the college of apostles. Therefore the pope and the other bishops must always work together. One bishop does not work independently of the others.

Governing The bishops are the chief authorities and pastors (shepherds) in the Church. Each bishop exercises authority in his diocese. He also shares a worldwide authority with the pope and the other bishops. In the diocese the bishop directs the life of the Church. He is the visible sign of its unity. He coordinates its work, he helps it to keep focused on its true mission of building God's kingdom, and he brings people of different backgrounds together in harmony. Like Christ the Good Shepherd, the bishop is to watch over all those under his care, especially the weak.

Sanctifying The bishop has the fullness of the sacrament of Holy Orders. He is the chief priest of the diocese and shares this priesthood with the presbyters, whom he ordains. With these coworkers he sanctifies the Church through prayer and the ministry of both word and sacrament, especially the Eucharist. Through the bishop we are reminded that the Eucharist is the center of the life of the Church.

At every Mass, we mention by name the bishop of the diocese. Next time you hear your bishop's name at Mass, remember how challenging his ministry is and pray for him.

What do these pictures tell us about the work of a bishop?

The Church of Christ

A correct understanding of the Church is so important for Catholics that it was one of the major topics of the Second Vatican Council. After long reflection and discussion, the bishops, who had gathered from every part of the world, gave us a deep insight into the meaning of the Church. They taught that the Church of Christ, the Church founded upon Christ and the apostles, is made up of a number of "elements." Without these basic elements there would be no Church.

First and foremost the Church is one, holy, catholic, and apostolic. These characteristics are essential features of the Church. But there are other elements that are essential to the Church, too. These include both visible and invisible elements.

The *visible elements*, as the name suggests, are those that make the Church a recognizable body in the world. After all, the Church is an organization of people with leaders, beliefs, laws, and practices. This organization can be readily seen and recognized by all. Among the vital elements of the Church that make it visible, the council bishops mentioned the following:

- Scripture, which is the Church's written record of God's revelation. Scripture cannot be changed or ignored because it is a permanent document.
- Baptism, along with the other sacraments of the Church. Remember that no one can become a member of the Church without first having been baptized.
- Episcopacy, which is the office of bishop. This includes the pope, the bishop of Rome. Episcopacy links the Church through the apostles to Christ himself.
- Eucharist, which is the source and high point of the Church's life.
- Doctrines of faith, which are the teachings that come down to us from the time of the apostles.
- Devotion to Mary, the Mother of God. Her spiritual motherhood extends to all the members of the Church.

The *invisible elements* have to do with the Church's inner life. As the name suggests, the elements cannot be seen except in their results. The members of the Church show these elements by the way they live. Among the vital elements of the Church that cannot be seen, the council bishops mentioned the following:

- The life of grace, which is a participation in the very life of God.
- The theological virtues of faith, hope, and love, which are gifts from God. They are powers enabling us to act as children of God.
- The gifts of the Holy Spirit, who is continually sanctifying the Church.

CATHOLIC TEACHINGS

About the Gifts of the Holy Spirit

The Church teaches that there are seven gifts of the Holy Spirit and that these are part of the invisible elements of the Church. These gifts are wisdom, understanding, right judgment, courage, knowledge, reverence, and wonder and awe. Through these gifts we become open to the promptings of the Holy Spirit in our lives.

The Catholic Church

Look again at the elements of the Church. Each must be present in Christ's Church. And where do we find that Church of Christ? The bishops of the council gave a clear answer. They said that the Church of Christ can be found in its essential fullness in the Catholic Church. This is what they taught:

> This is the unique Church of Christ which in the Creed we avow as one, holy, catholic, and apostolic. . . . This Church, constituted and organized in the world as a society, subsists in the Catholic Church, which is governed by the successor of Peter and by the bishops in union with that successor, although many elements of sanctification and of truth can be found outside her visible structure.
> *Church*, 8

The council teaching is that the Church of Christ "subsists" in the Catholic Church. This means that the Church of Christ is truly present in its essential completeness in the Catholic Church. However, as the bishops pointed out, some of the elements of the Church are present in other Christian Churches and communities. For example, all Christians accept and revere Scripture. All Christians are received into the body of Christ through Baptism and enjoy the life of sanctifying grace. Not all Christians, however, continue fully in the apostolic life of the Church under the leadership of the pope and bishops, the successors of the apostles. Nor do all of them have the seven sacraments.

What does this council teaching about the Catholic Church have to do with our daily lives? Everything! That is why we will spend the next lesson trying to understand its importance.

 Try to learn by heart both the visible and the invisible elements of the Church.

Second Vatican Council, 1962–1965

Something Special

If somebody asked you to give the best definition of a precious jewel, such as an emerald, it would not be an easy task. That is because there would be so much to say about the luster and beauty of the gem, its many sides and reflective powers. So it is with the Catholic Church. It, too, has so many aspects that it is difficult to capture all of them in just a few words. However, based on what we have already studied, we can begin to build a helpful definition of the Catholic Church.

We can say that the *Catholic Church* is the community of those who follow Jesus Christ, the community that:

- professes belief in Jesus Christ, the Son of God and risen Lord
- publicly affirms its belief in Christ through Baptism
- celebrates that faith through the Eucharist and other sacraments
- accepts the teachings of Christ that have come down from the time of the apostles
- carries out the sacramental life and mission of the Church under the leadership of those ordained in apostolic succession, that is, the pope and other bishops, together with their priests and deacons.

This definition of the Catholic Church summarizes the key elements of the Church of Christ, both visible and invisible. This is the Church that we experience in our local parish and diocese. This is the Church that we experience when we gather together around the Lord's table to celebrate the Eucharist. This is the Church that exists all over the world. This is also the Church that receives from Christ our Savior "the fullness of the means of salvation" (*Catechism*, 830).

Can there be any doubt, then, that the Catholic Church is something special and that we are privileged to be members of it?

Practical Matters

Knowing how special it is to be a Catholic, we need to ask an important question: What is our relationship to other Christians? Catholics should make no mistake about it. We accept all other Christians as our brothers and sisters in Christ. The Second Vatican Council taught that the Catholic Church accepts other Christians "with respect and affection" (*Ecumenism*, 3).

Nevertheless we do not believe that the Catholic Church and other Christian Churches are all the same. There are differences in belief, practice, and

Church organization that separate us. We do not share unity now, but it is our hope that one day all of Christ's followers will be united as one. This is the hard work of ecumenism. *Ecumenism* refers to the effort on the part of Catholics and other Christians to work toward full unity among all baptized people around the world.

To achieve unity, we try to pray and work together with other Christians. But true unity can never be attained if we ignore the real differences that separate us. Take the Eucharist, for example. Unlike some other Christians, Catholics believe that Christ is truly present in the Eucharist and that the Eucharist is a sign of unity. That is why those who do not share our faith are not invited to receive Communion when they visit and attend our celebrations of the Mass. The reception of Holy Communion is a sign of the unity we have in faith, life, and worship within our Catholic community. To share Communion with those not

united with us would deny what is really true—that we are not yet one in faith.

In the same way Catholics may not receive communion in Churches that do not share with us our belief in the real presence and that do not have the sacrament of Holy Orders or the apostolic succession of bishops. Without these vital elements we cannot accept their communion as a valid sacrament. To do so would be to deny our belief in the sacramental system of the Church.

There are other occasions as well when we will need to look carefully at the special nature of our Catholic life and faith. Take, for example, marriage between Catholics and non-Catholics. The Church asks the couple planning such a marriage to spend serious time in thought and preparation before taking this important step. The Church, while respecting the faith of the non-Catholic party, asks the Catholic to reaffirm his or her faith. In addition the Catholic is asked to do all in his or her power to see that the children of this marriage are brought up as Catholics. This makes sense, of course. If being a member of the Catholic Church is so important, then all Catholics will want to share their faith with their children.

 Think of some ways that you can grow in a deeper appreciation of your Catholic faith.

Scripture UPDATE

If anything is clear in the gospels, it is the close relationship Christ had with his apostles. They were the foundation upon which he built his Church. Our link to Christ and his mission is through the bishops, the successors to the apostles. This apostolic succession of the bishops is an important part of the apostolic succession of the whole Church.

things
to think about

What does it mean for you to know that our bishops are the Church's links to the apostles and to Christ himself?

Why should we, as Catholics, listen to our bishops when they speak about issues that affect us today?

things
to share

Imagine that you as a Catholic have been invited to a cousin's wedding. Your cousin is not a Catholic, and the ceremony will be held at a Protestant church. Your cousin hopes that you will not only attend but also receive communion at the ceremony. What would you say to help your cousin understand what you will do?

Someone says to you that ecumenism demands that Christian Churches should discuss only those things they agree on or share and should avoid any difficult topics. Your response?

WORDS TO REMEMBER

Find and define the following:

visible elements of the Church_____
_____
_____

invisible elements of the Church_____
_____
_____

OnLine
WITH THE PARISH

Each year the Church sets aside a week to pray for Christian unity. However, our parishes can pray and work for unity throughout the year. What do you think young people your age can do to contribute to the ecumenical movement in your neighborhood? Brainstorm several ideas.

1. Give the most complete definition of the Catholic Church that you can.

2. Explain this statement of Saint Cyprian: "The bishop is in the Church and the Church in the bishop."

3. Name and explain two visible elements of the Church of Christ.

4. What do we mean when we speak of the threefold ministry?

5. Define ecumenism and explain its importance for the Church.

Life in the Spirit

Suppose that one hundred years from now someone is going to describe what kind of Catholic you were, what it meant to you to be a member of the Church. What would you like that person to say about you? After you finish your description, make it a part of your prayer this week. For example, you might say, "God, help me to grow and become this strong member of your Church."

CATHOLICISM:
A WAY OF LIFE

You are "a chosen race, a royal priesthood, a holy nation, a people of his own."

1 Peter 2:9

ARE you an important member of the Church? Does what you do really make a difference? What do you think?

The Laity

Something wonderful happens when people are baptized and become members of the Church. From that very moment they are changed forever. At Baptism we become not only new creations in Christ and share in God's own life, but we are called to a new way of life. We are called to join in the mission of Christ to the world.

How do Catholics live this new way of life? Basically in one of three ways: Some people become members of religious orders and communities. Others are called to live as ordained ministers. But most of the baptized live their Catholic lives as members of the laity—that is, as laypeople.

As laypeople our way of life begins in and revolves around the parish. There we receive the sacraments of initiation: Baptism, Confirmation, and Eucharist. There we celebrate the sacrament of Reconciliation for the first time. In the parish we continue our instruction in faith that was begun by our parents. We learn more about Jesus, his Church, and what it means to be a Catholic in today's challenging world.

Years later we may celebrate the sacrament of Matrimony in our parish church and begin to journey down a new path in life. It is in the parish as well that we say farewell for the last time to those we love at the celebration of a Christian funeral. Truly the parish is our home in the Catholic Church from the first moment of our lives until the last.

The sacramental life and religious instruction are truly important, but parish life doesn't end there. A parish offers many opportunities for the laity to serve Christ. That is why the first thing that Catholics do when they move into a neighborhood is to register in, or join, the local parish. By adding their names and addresses to the list of parishioners, they become part of the local Catholic family.

It is in the parish that Catholics discover many opportunities to serve others. All their talents can be used in one way or another in various parish committees, organizations, or ministries. For example, laymen and laywomen may be called to serve on the parish council or finance committee. Others may become involved in religious education or take up the work of sharing faith with others in programs of Christian initiation.

Many people feel called to various outreach programs in a parish. These include ministry to the sick or homebound and to those in need of food, clothing, or shelter. Others find that they can serve through involvement with the liturgy. They help to plan liturgies and participate in the liturgical celebrations in their roles as altar servers, members of choirs, leaders of song, musicians, lectors, and extraordinary ministers of the Eucharist.

Some laypeople travel halfway around the globe to serve as missionaries in other lands. Others do mission work in our own country, serving wherever the need is the greatest. Today more than ever before, qualified laypeople are taking leadership positions in dioceses and local parishes. Working closely with the bishop, priests, and deacons, laypeople are putting their talents to work in many ways.

In recent times the Holy Spirit has renewed our understanding of the dignity and importance of the laity in the Church. Now more than ever before the laity are sharing in pastoral ministry as team members. It is exciting to see.

While all this is true, we know that the majority of laypeople carry on the mission of the Church each day by sharing the good news of Christ in the workplace. They use their gifts in their occupations and professions to change the world by the light of the gospel. In all they do, they try to bring to their surroundings the love and justice that is characteristic of God's kingdom.

Jesus himself sent disciples other than the Twelve to join in his saving mission and to prepare the way for him. He once sent out seventy-two to many towns. He reminded them, "The harvest is abundant but the laborers are few; so ask the master of the harvest to send out laborers for his harvest" (Luke 10:2).

 Discuss some ways that young people can serve the Church in their parishes.

Religious

Although the laity are the largest group of people in the Church, many thousands of Catholics live out their lives in a different way. These are the members of religious orders and communities. How did this way of life come about?

Throughout the history of the Church, certain men and women have tried to follow Christ in a special way. These are people such as Benedict, Francis of Assisi, Elizabeth Seton, and Teresa of Calcutta. So attractive are their lives and relationships with God that many people have wanted to imitate them. Communities developed around these holy people. Eventually the Church reviewed their way and rules of life and approved them as religious orders and communities. Today these communities are spread throughout the world. How do they live, and what do they do? Let's look more closely at this unique way of living the Catholic life.

Evangelical Counsels   Religious men and women consecrate themselves to God by vowing to practice poverty, chastity, and obedience. These are known as the *evangelical counsels* because they reflect a gospel way of life. By living these counsels, religious try to follow Christ's example.

- *Poverty* means that a religious man or woman owns no property and tries to live a simple lifestyle. Without seeking wealth or status, a religious gives witness to our total dependence on God and our deep respect for the proper use of this world's goods.

- *Chastity* means that a religious man or woman lives a life of purity as a witness to the kingdom of God. It includes a life of celibacy, which means not marrying. In trying to imitate Jesus in this way, religious want to be free to share God's love with the greatest number of people.

- *Obedience* means that religious men and women choose to listen carefully to God's direction in their lives. Obedience to the Church and to their religious superior means that individual religious are ready to serve God and the Church anywhere.

All religious share in the joy of community life, ministry, and prayer.

Community Life   The vowed life of religious is not easy, but it is filled with joy. The vows themselves are positive ways of following Christ's example. The close bonds that religious form in their own community enable them to live their vows fully each day. This is what we mean by a community life. The religious community is truly an individual's religious family.

Some communities are made up of vowed men who also become priests. Some communities are made up of vowed women, whom we call religious sisters. Still others are made up of vowed men who do not become priests. They are known as religious brothers.

Contemplative or Active   There are differences among religious communities. In *contemplative religious communities* men and women dedicate themselves entirely to a life of prayer. They willingly separate themselves from the busyness of the world. They pray constantly for all the members of the Church, but their lives remain hidden from us. That is why they are called contemplatives. In many ways these men and women are the powerhouses of prayer for the entire Church. You may know of some contemplative religious communities, such as the Trappists, the Poor Clares, and the Carmelites.

Active religious communities combine a life of prayer with a life of active service. They take part in all aspects of the Church's life. They sponsor and staff schools and hospitals, serve as missionaries, give retreats, work in parishes, and engage in many other ministries. Wherever there is a need in the Church, active religious are ready to go. You may know of some active communities, such as the Jesuits, Franciscan men and women, the Sisters of Mercy, and the Marist Brothers.

Religious communities come in all shapes and sizes. Some have a long history; some are very recent. No matter what, these communities are one of God's great blessings to the Church.

What qualifications do you think a person needs to join a religious community?

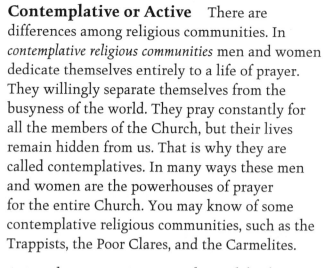

CATHOLIC ID There are two kinds of priests. A *religious priest* is a member of a religious order or community and professes the vows of poverty, chastity, and obedience. He serves anywhere in the world his superiors assign him. A *diocesan priest* is ordained for a particular diocese. With the bishop he dedicates his life to the care of the people of that diocese. He is not a religious nor does he profess the vows of a religious. A diocesan priest does, however, make a promise of celibacy. He also promises obedience to his bishop.

Msgr. Hartman and Rabbi Gellman on Good Morning America

Clergy

The membership of the Catholic Church is made up of laity, religious, and clergy. Everyone in the Church belongs to one of these groups. Each group is an important part of our Catholic way of life.

The clergy make up the ordained leadership of the Church. These are the bishops, priests (presbyters), and deacons who are empowered by God to exercise authority in the Church. They do this for the service of God's people, each according to his rank in the sacrament of Holy Orders.

The clergy dedicate their lives to the work of Christ and his Church. The priest is the coworker of the bishop in the work of teaching, governing, and sanctifying. Priests, therefore, are never to work independently of the bishop. Rather, they are his representatives in the pastoral care of God's people. Although deacons do not share in the priesthood, as bishops and priests do, they are ordained for a ministry of service.

What about other titles of the clergy, such as cardinal, archbishop, and monsignor? These titles are given to bishops and priests who carry on a special work for the Church or as a special honor. Cardinals and archbishops are bishops; monsignors are priests.

The pope himself is a bishop, the bishop of Rome. As the successor of Peter, he is the head of the college of bishops. In fact the pope has supreme authority over the whole Church. He can make decisions independently of the other bishops but not against or apart from them. This is because the pope and all the other bishops are united in a sacred college.

Official Teachers

In the Church the official teachers with full authority—the authority of Christ himself—are the pope and the other bishops. They are the official teachers for the whole Church. We call them the *magisterium*, from the Latin word for "teacher."

The teaching office of the magisterium is carried out in two ways. The *ordinary magisterium* is the day-to-day teaching of the pope and bishops about the truths of our faith. Sometimes, however, the pope and bishops teach in a very solemn and formal way. This is called the *extraordinary magisterium*. It happens when the pope gathers all the bishops of the world together at an ecumenical (worldwide) council. Or it happens when the pope by himself makes a solemn and extraordinary pronouncement about our faith.

Jesus promised to be with his Church always, even to the end of the world. He sent the Holy Spirit to teach it and preserve it in the truth (John 16:13). That is why it is unthinkable that the Church, the body of Christ, could fall into error in matters of faith and morality. This is a great gift to the Church.

Catholics have a special name for this gift. That name is infallibility. *Infallibility* is the gift of the Holy Spirit that keeps the whole Church from error—in believing and in teaching—in matters concerning revelation and the deposit of faith. This is the divine guarantee we have that the Church can never be in error about the truths necessary for our salvation.

How is the gift of infallibility exercised in the official teaching office of the Church? It happens only in teaching about matters of faith and morals:

- when the bishops, spread around the world in their own dioceses and in union with the pope, teach the truths of our faith with one voice.
- when the bishops of the world, gathered together by the pope in an ecumenical council, define a truth of our faith.
- when the pope speaks to the whole Church on a matter of faith and morals with the full authority he has as successor of Saint Peter. When the pope does this, he is speaking, not as an individual bishop, but as the pastor of the whole Church. This exercise of infallibility by the pope alone is rare.

What a wonderful thing it is to know that the Holy Spirit is guiding the Church!

Imagine that the Holy Father has called an ecumenical council and that it will begin in the near future. What do you think the world's bishops will talk about?

CATHOLIC TEACHINGS

About Infallibility

Does infallibility extend to all areas of knowledge? Absolutely not! It has to do only with matters of faith and morals. It has nothing to do with matters of science or other areas of human knowledge. You may be familiar with the story of Galileo. A long time ago the Church misunderstood the work of this great scientist. It mistakenly condemned his scientific teachings about the universe. Today, of course, we know better, and the Church has acknowledged its mistake. This kind of mistake, however, has nothing to do with the gift of infallibility.

A Communion of Churches

The Catholic Church's way of life is rich and diverse. As the people of God, Catholics are one, but this unity does not mean that we are all alike. Our Church spreads across every culture and includes many different peoples.

How did this wonderful diversity come to be? As the first Christian communities were founded during the apostolic age, many developed their own unique customs, laws, and practices. Later the Church spread across the Roman Empire. As the empire split into eastern and western sections, differences among the various Churches became more apparent. The Church of the West became known as the Latin, or Western, Catholic Church. The Churches of the East became known as the Eastern Catholic Churches.

The Eastern Catholic Churches should not be confused with the Eastern Orthodox Churches. The Orthodox Churches separated themselves from union with the pope in A.D. 1054 and are not part of the Catholic Church.

Although the Western Church and the Eastern Catholic Churches had many differences, their fundamental beliefs remained the same. Through apostolic succession each had seven sacraments, the threefold ministry (bishop, priest, and deacon), and the same creeds. All of them acknowledged the bishop of Rome, the successor of Peter, as the head of the Church.

Today the whole Catholic Church is made up of twenty-two distinct Catholic Churches in communion with one another and the bishop of Rome. Each of the twenty-two Churches observes one of the Rites of the Church. A *Rite* is a distinctive tradition of liturgy, laws, and customs that expresses the one Catholic faith in its own unique way. There are six different Rites that are practiced by the twenty-two Churches of the Catholic Church.

Most Catholics in the United States follow the Latin Rite. However, Latin Rite Catholics should realize that they can attend Mass (usually called the Divine Liturgy in Eastern Catholic Churches) in any of the other twenty-one Catholic Churches. They may also receive the sacraments there.

Pope John Paul II with a Byzantine Catholic bishop

Christ and His Church

Just as Jesus brought humanity the fullness of God, so the Church brings the fullness of Christ to the world. Jesus Christ, then, lives on in his Church. The Church is really like a sacrament; it makes Christ visible to the world. Jesus' mission is the mission of the Church. The kingdom of God that Jesus preached is the kingdom that the Church seeks to bring about. All this reminds us that the Church is necessary for our salvation, for it is there that we meet Christ our Savior.

Is the Church perfect? No, only God is perfect. Will the Church last? If the Church were merely of human origin, it would never last. But if it comes from God, no one can stop it (Acts 5:38–39). After two thousand years, no one has!

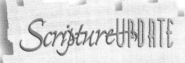

The Letter to the Colossians summarizes what it means to be a member of the Church: "Whatever you do, in word or in deed, do everything in the name of the Lord Jesus, giving thanks to God the Father through him" (3:17).

The accompanying chart lists the names of all twenty-two Churches and the Rites followed by each. It will help you to appreciate even more beauty and richness of the Catholic Church.

The Catholic Church	
Churches	**Rites**
1. Latin Catholic Church	This Church follows the Latin (Roman) Rite.
2. Belorussian Catholic Church 3. Bulgarian Catholic Church 4. Greek Catholic Church 5. Hungarian Catholic Church 6. Italo-Albanian Catholic Church 7. Melkite Catholic Church 8. Romanian Catholic Church 9. Ruthenian Catholic Church 10. Slovak Catholic Church 11. Ukrainian Catholic Church 12. Krizevci Catholic Church 13. Albanian Catholic Church 14. Russian Catholic Church	These thirteen Churches follow the Byzantine (Constantinopolitan) Rite.
15. Chaldean Catholic Church 16. Malabar Catholic Church	These two Churches follow the Chaldean Rite.
17. Coptic Catholic Church 18. Ethiopian Catholic Church	These two Churches follow the Alexandrian Rite.
19. Syrian Catholic Church 20. Maronite Catholic Church 21. Syro-Malankara Catholic Church	These three Churches follow the Antiochine Rite.
22. Armenian Catholic Church	This Church follows the Armenian Rite.

Try to find out where the homelands of some of these Churches are. For example, most Catholics in Lebanon belong to the Maronite Catholic Church.

things
to think about

Why do you think it is important for laity, religious, and clergy to work together in the Church?

In your opinion what are the most exciting ways that laypeople can serve in the Church?

things
to share

How would you go about explaining to someone that Catholicism is really a way of life?

Someone says to you that only priests, sisters, and brothers can be missionaries in the Church, not laypeople. What would you say in response?

WORDS TO REMEMBER

Find and define the following:

magisterium _____
_____
_____

infallibility _____
_____
_____

OnLine
WITH THE PARISH

Did you know that your name is officially inscribed in the Catholic Church? It is! In the parish where you were baptized, your name was written down in the parish records and will remain there. This parish is your "home base" in the Catholic Church. Whenever you need a copy of your baptismal certificate, you must contact that parish. Do you know in which parish you were baptized? Remember it always!

1. What do we mean when we say that the Catholic Church is a communion of Churches?

2. Name the three vows taken by religious men and women, and explain one of them.

3. What do we mean by the ordinary magisterium of the Church?

4. Why should we consider infallibility as a gift from God?

5. Name some of the ministries in which laypeople serve.

Life in the Spirit

We know that the Church is both human and divine. Sometimes, however, we may see too much of the human side of the Church when we hear about the mistakes and weaknesses of Church members—laity, religious, or clergy. What should we do? Christ has asked us to love one another, to support one another, and to pray for one another. In times of weakness we need to turn to our community for strength and nourishment. Think of all the times we can pray for one another, especially at Mass. Use these times to help build up the Church and to grow in love for the Church.

CHAPTER 14

THE CHURCH ON ITS WAY

For here we have no lasting city, but we seek the one that is to come.

Hebrews 13:14

WHAT dreams do you have for the future?
What dreams do you think God has for our future?

The Pilgrim Church

From the time of the apostles, the Church has been part of every age. It has grown and developed and spread around the world. It is here, but it is not yet complete. The Church is on its way: It is the pilgrim Church.

Why do we call it the pilgrim Church? The Church is like a pilgrim walking in Christ's footsteps in the world. On this pilgrimage we, the people of God, are invited to go along with Christ. He is headed toward the final stage of completing the Church. That stage takes us to the fulfillment of God's kingdom, when Jesus will bring us home with him forever. This pilgrimage, however, is not a free ride. Between today and the last day of the world, there is a great deal to be done to get the world ready for Christ. He is coming again.

The Last Day

Jesus' first coming was at his birth. His *second coming* will be at the end of the world. This second coming is also called the last day, or the day of judgment. The last day will be the end of the world and life as we know it. At that moment the whole magnificent plan of God will be complete. Everything will change. The world we know, with its clouds, mountains, city streets, and country roads, will no longer be the same. All the things we are concerned about now—falling in love, taking a test, getting ill, having fun, even death itself—will come to an end as we know them. Then Christ and his faithful followers will be united forever; the Church will be completed.

When will all this happen? Jesus did not say. It wasn't his Father's wish that he make that detail known. How will the world end? We aren't sure.

A timeless, changeless new world will be ours. It seems almost unimaginable, but words such as *time* and *change* will no longer have meaning for us. That's how different everything will be.

For those in heaven there will not be the least chance of being unhappy, lonely, uncertain, or troubled again in any way. What is heaven? *Heaven* is life with the Blessed Trinity forever. It is the state of supreme happiness in which those who have been faithful to God and his commandments will enjoy the beatific vision, seeing God "face-to-face." Jesus himself told us, "I will see you again, and your hearts will rejoice, and no one will take your joy away from you" (John 16:22).

Those in hell, on the other hand, will be miserable for all eternity. *Hell* is eternal separation from God. Hell is the just punishment for those who have rejected God. For those who deliberately choose a life of sin, there is nothing ahead but everlasting misery.

The choice we make between living for heaven or living for hell will be made known before the whole world on the last day, the day of judgment. On the day of judgment, everyone who ever lived will be present together. Then all will know where they stand in relation to one another and to Christ. This is the *last judgment* that will accompany Christ's second coming at the end of the world. It is described with powerful imagery in Scripture. On that day Jesus will come in glory as a king and judge, sitting on a throne surrounded by angels. Everyone who ever existed will be assembled before him. Those whom he has placed on his right will enjoy "eternal life"; those on his left will go off to "eternal punishment" (Matthew 25:31–46). The message is clear; the way we live our lives is up to us.

We know only that Jesus put us on alert. He said, "Stay awake, for you know neither the day nor the hour" (Matthew 25:13).

Should we be afraid of this last day and worry that everything will be destroyed? Not at all. God has promised us that it will be the beginning of new life, the likes of which we have never experienced. At his second coming Christ will take possession of creation for his Father and remake it. We read in 2 Peter 3:13: "According to his promise we await new heavens and a new earth."

When Christ comes, we shall see him for ourselves. What we believed without seeing will then become clear, and we will go on forever with the risen Christ, our brother and our Lord.

Do you ever think of yourself as a pilgrim? Where are you headed? Who goes with you? What hopes do you have about your destination?

For those who have served Christ, death will be the day they have been waiting for—the end of their earthly pilgrimage and the beginning of endless happiness and peace. Will this eternal happiness start immediately? No. For many there must first be a process of purification, which the Church calls purgatory. *Purgatory* is a process of final purification after death in which those who have died in the state of grace grow in the holiness they need to enter the joy of heaven. We can help the souls experiencing purgatory by our good works and prayers, especially the Mass. That is because the souls in purgatory are certain of heaven, unlike those who have chosen hell.

The day of death is final. On that day, in what is called the *particular judgment*, Christ will judge the choice each individual has made and will determine the eternal reward or punishment that each choice deserves. This choice and its consequence—heaven or hell—is what will be repeated before the whole world at the last judgment at the end of the world.

People of faith should not get nervous at the mention of heaven, hell, and judgment. Heaven actually begins on earth with Baptism and is completed in eternity. Because we trust in God's great love and mercy, the Church reminds us that staying out of hell is not our life's work. Staying in heaven is.

Our Personal Last Day

Human beings have a limited time on earth. Death is a part of our life; it is a result of original sin. In every person's life there is a "last day," and this last day takes place before Christ's second coming. This personal last day is the day we die.

At the time of our death, we shall see ourselves as we are. We will be judged on the choices we have made in the light of Christ's teachings. By the way we live now, we choose heaven or hell. Free people have to accept the responsibility and the consequences of their choices. God does not choose heaven or hell for any one of us; we choose it for ourselves.

CATHOLIC TEACHINGS

About Death

Even though death is a time of great sadness, Catholics have a sure hope in the resurrection. Everything we do points to this hope. We gather to support one another at a wake service and kneel at the coffin to pray for the deceased. Our funeral liturgy is filled with the good news of eternal life. We bury the body with reverence in blessed ground. We continue to pray for our loved ones after their death. We believe what we say in the liturgy: "Lord, for your faithful people life is changed, not ended."

The Resurrection of the Dead

Our profession of faith concludes with our belief in the resurrection of the dead on the last day. Catholics firmly proclaim that just as Christ rose from the dead, so will Christ raise us up. On the last day our souls will be reunited with our bodies. Jesus himself scolded some people who did not believe in the resurrection of the dead (Mark 12:24). Jesus also described himself as the "resurrection and the life" (John 11:25). Several times he even gave a sign of the future by bringing some of the dead back to life.

The resurrection of the body is difficult for some people to accept. After all, the body decays after burial, and some bodies are even cremated. What do we say about this? We respond in faith. Just as Christ rose from the dead with his human body totally transformed, so he promised that we will rise at the end of time with our bodies transformed. How will this happen? Through God's almighty power, which is beyond our imagination and understanding.

What we can say with certainty is that we belong completely to Christ. From the moment of Baptism, we are united with him, both body and soul. Because human beings are not just souls, both the body and the soul should experience the rewards or punishments of eternal life.

A Catholic View

You may have heard someone say, "In my next life, I want to be . . . ." What should a Catholic say to this? The Church's teachings about the last things are definite and clear and come from what God has revealed to us. After our pilgrimage of life on earth is ended, God will not make us live another earthly life or a series of earthly lives. We will die only once and then stand before the God of justice, mercy, and love. That is why Catholics do not believe in reincarnation. The idea is totally contrary to God's plan for us.

You may also have heard people who claim to know when and how the world will end. They quote passages from Scripture that seem to say the world will end in complete destruction, with stars and planets falling from the sky. What should a Catholic's reaction be?

As always we turn to the Church to guide us. Just as Catholics see the truth of creation described in poetic terms in Scripture, so, too, the end of time is described in a poetic but truthful way. God is not a God of destruction; he is a God of love. As we already know, there will be new heavens and a new earth. The Church really does have a beautiful and hope-filled view of the end of time and eternal life.

How should our beliefs in the last things affect our daily lives? Do these beliefs frighten you? challenge you? give you hope? Explain.

Who is this woman for whom thousands of parish churches are named and whose image we see in millions of statues and paintings throughout the world? Why do Catholics show her such great honor and devotion?

There has never been anyone quite like Mary. From all eternity God chose her to be the mother of his Son. For that reason God gave her the privilege of being free from original sin from the first moment of her conception in her mother's womb. This privilege of Mary is what we know as the *immaculate conception*. It doesn't mean that Mary wasn't fully human. It means that she experienced redemption from the first moment of her life. She was full of grace. This was appropriate because she was to be the mother of the Savior of the world. She would carry God's only Son in her womb for nine months.

How did Mary become the mother of God's only Son? At the annunciation she said yes to God's invitation, and she conceived through the power of the Holy Spirit. Her son was not conceived through sexual relations, as other children are. Jesus was to have no human father, but only his Father in heaven. That is why we call Joseph the foster father of Jesus. That is also why we call Mary a virgin and why Jesus' birth is described as a virgin birth. Mary never engaged in sexual relations at any time in her life.

As we already know, the child born of the Virgin Mary was a divine Person with both a human nature and a divine nature. For that reason the greatest title of Mary is Mother of God. Jesus was not a human person; he was a divine Person with two natures. And that is why the Church reminds us that Mary must always be seen in relationship to her son. Mary's greatness comes from Christ. The Church's teaching is clear: "What the Catholic faith believes about Mary is based on what it believes about Christ, and what it teaches about Mary illumines in turn its faith in Christ" (*Catechism*, 487).

The Morning Star

A study of the Church and what it means to live a Catholic way of life would be incomplete without mentioning Mary, the mother of Jesus. On earth her life was an example of the Church's pilgrimage of faith. In heaven she is the image of what the Church hopes to be. That is why she has been given the beautiful title of the "Morning Star" in the Litany of the Blessed Virgin Mary. She is a guiding light to the pilgrim Church on its way.

The First Disciple

Who knew Jesus better than Mary did? We know from Scripture that she was an intimate part of Jesus' life. She brought him into the world. Like other mothers, she was there as her child grew. She witnessed his public ministry and even stood at the foot of the cross. But her closeness to Jesus did not end there. Along with Jesus' disciples she became a witness to the resurrection and ascension. She also waited in prayerful anticipation for the coming of the Holy Spirit. All these things tell us that Mary was the first of Jesus' disciples. From the moment she agreed to the incarnation, she was a Christian before anyone else was.

Mary cooperated fully with God's grace and remained free of any personal sin her whole life long. She was obedient to whatever God asked of her, and she followed no one but her son. In bringing Jesus into the world and in living as she did, Mary is a true model for the Church. She gives the example all of us should follow. Because we are the body of Christ, Mary, the mother of Jesus, is the Mother of the Church and our mother, too.

Although we do not know all the details of Mary's earthly life, we can be sure that she was a treasured member of the early Christian community. But what became of Mary? The Church teaches that because of her immaculate conception, Mary was given another privilege at the end of her life. She anticipated the resurrection that all of us will experience. Mary was taken up, or assumed, both body and soul into heaven at the end of her earthly life. This is known as the *assumption*.

Jesus loved his mother very much and knew how important she would be for his Church. When he was dying on the cross, Jesus himself said to John, his beloved disciple, and to us, "Behold, your mother" (John 19:27). Having been taken up into heaven, Mary has not forgotten us. She is still Mother of the Church. She is the mother of each one of us.

 Some people have described Mary as the perfect disciple of Jesus. Give examples to show why this is so.

ScriptureUPDATE

Mark 3:31–35 and several other Scripture passages refer to the brothers and sisters of Jesus. If Mary was always a virgin, what do these passages mean? The Church teaches us that these passages are "not referring to other children of the Virgin Mary. In fact James and Joseph, 'brothers of Jesus,' are the sons of another Mary, a disciple of Christ, whom St. Matthew significantly calls 'the other Mary.' They are close relations of Jesus, according to an Old Testament expression" (*Catechism*, 500).

Help Along the Way

Whenever we think of the Blessed Virgin Mary, we should remember that she is the first and greatest among the saints. Who are these men and women called saints? Why are they so important in our Catholic life?

The word *saint* means "one who is holy." It was used in the early Church to describe all the baptized. They were called holy because through Baptism they had been given a share in the divine life. As time passed, however, *saint* was used more often for holy people who followed Christ in extraordinary and heroic ways. For example, the early martyrs, who shed their blood for the faith, were immediately recognized and honored as saints in the communities where they lived.

Eventually an official process was developed to help the entire Church community recognize those who had lived exceptional lives of faith. This process is called *canonization*. How does it work? First the name of a person considered to be worthy of the title saint is submitted to Church authorities.

Then a thorough investigation of this person's life is conducted. When this process is completed and positive results are found, the pope proclaims that person a saint. Now the new saint can be honored by all the members of the Church. We can follow his or her path to holiness.

Are all the saints in heaven canonized? Of course not. Millions upon millions of good and holy people, including members of our own families, have not been officially canonized by the Church but may well be in heaven. The saints who have been canonized are a gift to the whole Church. They have been set before us as heroes and heroines of faith.

The canonized saints are a great treasure. We honor them by remembering them in prayer and by setting aside special feast days to commemorate their lives. Besides this, we name shrines, churches, and other institutions after them and dedicate these structures to their memory. But there is one day during the year when all the saints, both canonized and not canonized, are honored. That day is November 1.

Every Catholic should know that the Church has its own body of laws called canon law. The word *canon* means an "official rule." The canons of the Church are formulated to guide the life of the Church. Questions they deal with include Church administration, the rights and obligations of the faithful, and the correct procedures for Catholic marriages and other acts of divine worship. There are 1,752 canons, or laws, in the *Code of Canon Law*. There is one code of canon law for the Western Catholic Church and another for the Eastern Catholic Churches.

Left to right: St. Martin de Porres, St. Cecilia, Blessed Kateri Tekakwitha, St. Isidore the Farmer

Whenever we think about saints, we are reminded that all the members of the Church are connected with one another through Baptism and faith. This includes three groups: the members of the Church on earth, those experiencing purgatory, and those who have already attained the blessedness of heaven. We call this union of all the Church members the communion of saints. The *communion of saints* is the unity and cooperation of the members of the Church on earth with those in heaven and in purgatory.

Why is this communion of saints so important for us? It reminds us that we can pray for the dead and assist them by our prayers. It also reminds us that Mary and the other saints can pray for us, or intercede for us with God. The saints are our brothers and sisters in faith. Through their prayers for us and by the example of their lives, they are powerful friends in helping the pilgrim Church on its way.

If you could choose any saint to be your special friend and companion on the way, who would it be? Why? What might you talk about or do together?

Living as Catholics

Our study of basic Catholic beliefs has now come to a close. Each day we have an opportunity to make these beliefs a part of our lives. Our beliefs are so important that they truly identify us as members of the Catholic Church.

Our beliefs give meaning to everything we do. What we believe about the life of grace and our need for salvation, for example, affects the choices we make between right and wrong. Knowing about the Blessed Trinity and understanding the importance of Christ and his Church are the foundations of our sacramental life and worship of God. Our understanding of God, revelation, and faith itself helps us to realize that we can have a personal relationship with the transcendent and living God. All our beliefs, in fact, shape our Catholic life each and every day.

As informed members of the Church today, we stand on the shoulders of those who have gone before us in faith. They have passed on to us the teachings of Christ and his Church and have shown us how to live them in a dynamic way. It is now up to us to share these with the whole world.

things to think about

What does it mean for you to know that you are a member of the communion of saints and connected with all the other members of the Church, living and dead?

Why do you think it is important for every Catholic to have a deep love and respect for the Blessed Virgin Mary?

things to share

Some people may say to us that the Catholic Church only looks backward. Knowing what you know about the pilgrim Church, what would you say?

Suppose people tell you that they know all about the end of the world. They claim that, according to the Bible, the end is coming next year. What would you say to them? Does the Bible give us the exact details about the end of the world?

WORDS TO REMEMBER

Find and define the following:

heaven _____
_____
_____

hell _____
_____
_____

purgatory_____
_____
_____

OnLine WITH THE PARISH

In many parishes, bells and chimes call people to worship, remind them of the time of day, and give praise to God. Very often at funerals, bells toll slowly and solemnly to honor the deceased person. Whenever you hear bells tolling during a funeral liturgy, remember that you, too, can pray for that person.

Explain the difference between the last judgment and the particular judgment.

1

Why was it appropriate for Jesus to have been born of a virgin mother?

2

What is the difference between the virgin birth and the immaculate conception?

3

What do Catholics believe about the resurrection of the dead?

4

What is the Catholic response to reincarnation?

5

Life in the Spirit

The Blessed Virgin Mary is so important for the Church that we honor her on many days during the liturgical year. Three of them are celebrated as holy days of obligation: the Immaculate Conception (December 8); Mary, Mother of God (January 1); and the Assumption (August 15). We can reflect on many of Mary's titles by praying the Litany of the Blessed Virgin Mary. Get a copy of this beautiful prayer, and try to pray it often.

CHAPTER 15

BRINGING THE WORLD
TO CHRIST

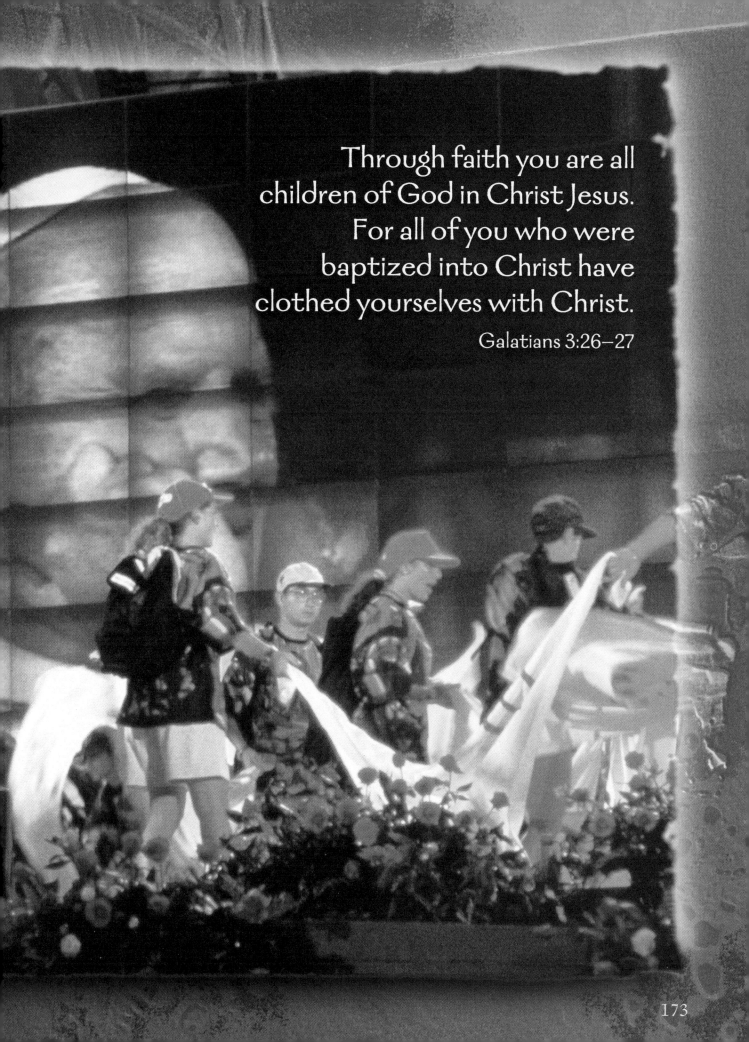

Through faith you are all children of God in Christ Jesus. For all of you who were baptized into Christ have clothed yourselves with Christ.

Galatians 3:26–27

THE day of our Baptism is a day unlike any other. From the moment of Baptism, we are changed forever. As children of God we are set apart and consecrated to carry on Christ's mission. Do you know the facts about your own Baptism? See how much of your baptismal record you can fill out from memory. Then ask your family to help.

My Baptismal Record

I,_____

the child of_____

and_____

and born on_____
          (date)

in_____
          (place)

was reborn in the sacrament of Baptism by water and the Holy Spirit

on_____
          (date)

by_____
          (priest or deacon)

in_____
          (parish community)

_____
          (address)

My sponsors were_____

and_____

Chosen by God

When does our responsibility to carry on Christ's mission to the whole world begin? Some people may think that this responsibility begins when we are adults or that it is something for older members of the Church. But that is not true. Recall the story of the prophet Jeremiah.

Jeremiah was a young man when God called him to be a prophet. In response to this call, Jeremiah said to God, "I know not how to speak; I am too young." At this God said to him, "Say not, 'I am too young.' To whomever I send you, you shall go; whatever I command you, you shall speak" (Jeremiah 1:6–7).

God is saying the same thing to each one of us in Christ. As people of faith and as members of the body of Christ, we are appointed right now to share our faith and the good news of the gospel with the whole world. We call this mission of bringing the good news to others evangelization.

Evangelization means bringing the good news to every person and to all parts of the human experience. It means that we bring the world to Christ and Christ to the world. It is something so exciting that when it happens, the lives of people are transformed from within and made new. They begin to see everything with the eyes of Christ.

This does not happen automatically. Rather, it takes initiative, commitment, and hard work. After all, the best witness to Christ and our faith is the way we live our lives. It takes more than good will and intention; we must know Christ and know our faith. That is one of the reasons this course on the creed is so important.

How can you as a young person carry on the work of evangelization? Where will you go? What will you do? Let's begin to explore three areas in which evangelization can happen: at home, in your school and neighborhood, and in the wider world. This will be a journey of discovery. Let us turn to the Holy Spirit and ask him to be our guide.

Looking at Ourselves

Evangelization is so important in the lives of Catholics that our recent popes have talked to us about it many times. But they do not want us to go off unprepared. Like Jesus they have urged us to look at the "signs of the times" (Matthew 16:3) to see where God wants us to work in our world, calling us to be a part of his kingdom.

The first people to be evangelized must be ourselves. Pope Paul VI, for example, said that "the first means of evangelization is the witness of an authentically Christian life" (*On Evangelization*, 41). This means that we have to believe and practice what we are going to share with others. Otherwise our witness becomes empty and unbelievable.

What are the signs of the times in your own life? Let's take a closer look. For example, think about the music you enjoy. What are your favorite songs? Write several of their titles here.

Why are these songs your favorites? What do the words of the songs tell you about yourself, what you hope for, what you enjoy? Do the words and feelings of these songs help you to live your faith? Do they make you uneasy about your faith?

The answers we give to questions such as these help us to see where faith challenges us. They help us to see where we must allow the gospel and all that we profess about our faith to become real for our lives. Remember Paul's words: "Through faith you are all children of God in Christ Jesus. For all of you who were baptized into Christ have clothed yourselves with Christ" (Galatians 3:26–27).

Do the things you enjoy, such as music, help you to see where you need to clothe yourself in Christ even more? How can your faith become more real in your life? Write your thoughts here.

Family Life

Once we have evangelized ourselves, the first and most obvious people with whom we come into contact are members of our family. Evangelizing, however, doesn't mean that we are going to preach to our family or tell them what to do. What it means is that we are going to try as hard as we can to bring the presence of Christ into our family's life in any way possible. What are the signs of the times in your family's life? Let's take a closer look.

Complete the following statements for yourself:

1. I most enjoy being with my family when

2. The quality I like best about my family is

3. I am most uncomfortable with my family when

4. My family is most uncomfortable with me when

In the chart check off the areas in which you think you need to grow or to work harder as a family evangelizer.

___ *gratitude*	___ *generosity*
___ *joy*	___ *anger*
___ *friendliness*	___ *patience*
___ *helpfulness*	___ *cheerfulness*
___ *enthusiasm*	___ *support*
___ *selfishness*	___ *stubbornness*
___ *jealousy*	___ *prayerfulness*
___ *cooperation*	___ *attentiveness*
___ *responsibility*	___ *forgiveness*

Look over your list and your answers. This isn't an examination of conscience or a way to find out how bad we are. This is a way to get in touch with our lives. This is a way to be real evangelizers, to bring the values of the gospel home with us.

The signs of the times are there for us to read. The possibilities of being effective evangelizers are there for us, too. Use this prayer to help you see more clearly how this can be done:

Jesus,
you have chosen me
as a member of your Church
to be your evangelizer.
Help me to
see each day where I can
bring the message
of your good news to others.
Help me to
transform my own life
and so be a witness
to my family.
Amen.

177

> *Young people who are*
> *well trained in faith and prayer*
> *must become more and more the apostles of youth.*
> *The Church counts greatly*
> *on their contribution.*
>
> *Pope Paul VI, On Evangelization, 72*

Friends

Having good friends is one of the greatest experiences we can ever have in life. Being good friends means that we wish only what is good for the other person — only what will make that person truly happy.

To help us get in touch with friendship, let's take a look at the way friendship is shown in our favorite movies and television programs.

Look over the answers you have written down in these charts. Are you surprised at your answers? How would you compare these answers with what your faith tells you about friendship? Friends can be evangelizers to one another. Do you see any possibility for evangelization here? Write a friendship evangelization plan.

My Friendship Evangelization Plan

Recent Movies I Have Seen

Names of Movies:

What These Movies Tell Me About Friendship:

Favorite Television Programs

Names of Television Programs:

What These Programs Tell Me About Friendship:

School and Neighborhood

Strange as it may seem, the hardest and most challenging place to be an effective evangelizer may very well be in our own backyard. It is always most difficult to evangelize our peers. It may be easier to travel halfway around the world and meet people who have never heard of Christ than to speak with and give witness to him among the people we see and hang out with day after day.

What does this mean? It means that we have to be courageous, imaginative, and skillful in bringing the truth and values of the gospel to this important part of our world. But how do we bring the gospel and the truth of faith to the football or soccer field, to the basketball court, to the mall, to the classroom, or to a Friday night dance? After all, this is the world in which we live every day.

Read the following descriptions, and think about the situations as possible evangelizing opportunities. For each, write one way you would try to bring gospel values to this experience.

The Church has so much to talk about with youth, and youth have so much to share with the Church.

Pope John Paul II
The Lay Faithful, 46

Evangelizing Moments

- For many months your parish council has been asking for volunteers of all ages to help start an outreach program to the elderly and the homebound. It is not easy to volunteer alone. What are your plans as an evangelizer?

- Sports have always been important in your school. But lately you and others have noticed a different attitude on the part of many, both young people and adults. Sports and winning seem to have taken over as the most important things in life. What are your plans as an evangelizer?

- The local mall is the place to hang out and meet others. However, the mall security guards have been cracking down in the last couple of months. People were complaining about the noise and rough behavior on the part of some of your peers. What are your plans as an evangelizer?

Look back at what you have written today about being an evangelizer. Are you surprised that evangelization can take place in situations where you might have thought it would not be possible?

A Young Evangelizer Writes

During my senior year at Georgetown University, one of my Jesuit teachers suggested that I volunteer to work in South Africa after graduation. I imagine he thought it would be a good way to round out my education as a Catholic and challenge me as a person of faith. Although his suggestion sounded exciting, I had some other ideas about my life. My life was filled with many blessings, and I wanted to give something back to my own community in the United States. That's how I ended up spending a year in a large U.S. city far from my home. There I taught young people in an inner-city school.

My experience opened my eyes to a part of life I had never really seen. In an area overrun with gangs, drugs, and violence, the strength and ability of my students impressed me deeply. I started out thinking that I could give something back to the community, but I was the one who was actually taught. Now as a law student I am learning to bring greater justice to the inner city.

Tom Sweeney

Another Young Evangelizer Writes

When I was in college, I had the opportunity to visit other countries in Central and South America. There I was shocked to see so many people living in cardboard houses and going hungry. For the first time in my life, I realized just how the poor of the world have to live. As a person of faith and a member of the Church, I knew that I had to do something about this.

After college I volunteered to work with a group sponsored by the Ursuline Sisters. This group is called Ursuline Companions in Mission. For the next two years, I found myself working alongside others in youth and prison ministry and family counseling here in the United States. I even went to Central America and worked in an orphanage in Honduras. Was it easy? No. But these experiences helped to change my life. Now as a teacher I try to share with young Catholics and help them see what missionary activity is all about.

Patrice McDermott

The Wider World

You may be surprised where life leads you as an evangelizer. For some it could even be halfway around the world. That's because the work of evangelization and mission is the work of all Church members, not just the clergy and religious. The Church teaches us that through Baptism we are a prophetic and priestly people offering spiritual sacrifices in our lives and announcing Christ to the world. The Church reminds us that "the faithful exercise their baptismal priesthood through their participation, each according to his own vocation, in Christ's mission as priest, prophet, and king" (Catechism, 1546).

Now that you have read about their experiences, what questions would you ask these two young Catholics about their evangelizing activities?

What dreams do you have for evangelizing in the wider world?

How can you prepare to help make those dreams come true?

181

A Prayer for Evangelizers

Leader: On the day of our Baptism, we began a journey of bringing the world to Christ. From that moment we have learned about our faith in Christ and are proud to profess it in his name. Before we renew our baptismal vows, let us listen closely to the word of God.

Reader 1: A reading from the First Letter of Peter:

You have tasted that the Lord is good. Come to him, a living stone, rejected by human beings but chosen and precious in the sight of God, and, like living stones, let yourselves be built into a spiritual house to be a holy priesthood to offer spiritual sacrifices acceptable to God through Jesus Christ. You are "a chosen race, a royal priesthood, a holy nation, a people of his own, so that you may announce the praises" of him who called you out of darkness into his wonderful light. Once you were "no people" but now you are God's people.
(1 Peter 2:3–5, 9–10)

The word of the Lord.

All: Thanks be to God.

Leader: Now let us renew our baptismal vows that were first made on the day of our Baptism.

Reader 2: Do you reaffirm your renunciation of evil and renew your commitment to Jesus Christ?

All: I do.

Reader 3: Do you believe in God the Father?

All: I believe in God, the Father almighty, creator of heaven and earth.

Reader 4: Do you believe in Jesus Christ, the Son of God?

All: I believe in Jesus Christ, his only son, our Lord.
He was conceived by the power of the Holy Spirit and born of the Virgin Mary.
He suffered under Pontius Pilate, was crucified, died, and was buried.
He descended to the dead.
On the third day he rose again.
He ascended into heaven, and is seated at the right hand of the Father.
He will come again to judge the living and the dead.

Reader 5: Do you believe in the Holy Spirit?

All: I believe in the Holy Spirit,
the holy catholic Church,
the communion of saints,
the forgiveness of sins,
the resurrection of the body,
and the life everlasting.

Reader 6: Will you continue in the apostles'
teaching and fellowship,
in the breaking of bread, and in
the prayers?

All: I will, with God's help.

Reader 7: Will you persevere in resisting evil,
and, whenever you fall into sin,
repent and return to the Lord?

All: I will, with God's help.

Reader 8: Will you proclaim by word and example
the Good News of God in Christ?

All: I will, with God's help.

Reader 9: Will you seek and serve Christ
in all persons,
loving your neighbor as yourself?

All: I will, with God's, help.

Reader 10: Will you strive for justice
and peace among all people,
and respect the dignity of every
human being?

All: I will, with God's, help.

Leader: May Almighty God,
the Father of our Lord Jesus Christ,
who has given us a new birth by water and
the Holy Spirit,
and bestowed upon us the forgiveness of sins,
keep us in eternal life by his grace,
in Christ Jesus our Lord.

All: Amen.

*Before singing a closing song, each member of the group
comes forward to dip his or her hand in holy water and
make the sign of the cross.*

IN THE NAME
OF THE FATHER,
and of the Son,
and of the Holy Spirit.
Amen.

SIGN OF THE CROSS

GLORY TO THE FATHER,
AND TO THE SON,
and to the Holy Spirit:
as it was in the beginning, is now,
and will be for ever.
Amen.

GLORY TO THE FATHER

O MY GOD,
I FIRMLY BELIEVE THAT
you are one God in three divine
Persons, Father, Son, and Holy Spirit;
I believe that your divine Son
became man and died for our sins,
and that he will come to
judge the living and the dead.
I believe these and all the
truths which the holy
Catholic Church teaches,
because you revealed them,
who can neither deceive
nor be deceived. Amen.

ACT OF FAITH

COME, HOLY SPIRIT,
FILL THE HEARTS OF YOUR FAITHFUL.
And kindle in them the fire of your love.

Send forth your Spirit and they shall be created.
And you will renew the face of the earth.

Let us pray.

Lord,
by the light of the Holy Spirit
you have taught the hearts of your faithful.
In the same Spirit
help us to relish what is right
and always rejoice in your consolation.

We ask this through Christ our Lord.
Amen.

PRAYER TO THE HOLY SPIRIT

ETERNAL REST
GRANT UNTO THEM,
O Lord.
And let perpetual light shine upon them.
May they rest in peace.
Amen.
May their souls and the souls of all the
faithful departed, through the mercy of
God, rest in peace.
Amen.

May the angels lead you into paradise;
may the martyrs come to welcome you
and take you to the holy city,
the new and eternal Jerusalem.

PRAYERS FOR THE DECEASED

184

O MY GOD, I LOVE YOU ABOVE ALL THINGS,

with my whole heart and soul,
because you are all good and worthy
of all my love. I love my neighbor
as myself for the love of you.
I forgive all who have injured me
and I ask pardon of all whom
I have injured. Amen.

ACT OF LOVE

O MY GOD, RELYING ON YOUR INFINITE

goodness and promises, I hope to
obtain pardon of my sins,
the help of your grace, and life
everlasting, through the merits
of Jesus Christ, my Lord and
Redeemer. Amen.

ACT OF HOPE

HAIL MARY, FULL OF GRACE,

the Lord is with you!
Blessed are you among women,
and blessed is the fruit of your womb,
 Jesus.
Holy Mary, Mother of God,
pray for us sinners,
now and at the hour of our death.
Amen.

HAIL MARY

I BELIEVE IN GOD, THE FATHER ALMIGHTY,

creator of heaven and earth.
I believe in Jesus Christ, his only Son,
  our Lord.
He was conceived by the power of
  the Holy Spirit
  and born of the Virgin Mary.
He suffered under Pontius Pilate,
  was crucified, died, and was buried.
He descended to the dead.
On the third day he rose again.
He ascended into heaven,
  and is seated at the right hand
  of the Father.
He will come again to judge the living
  and the dead.
I believe in the Holy Spirit,
  the holy catholic Church,
  the communion of saints,
  the forgiveness of sins,
  the resurrection of the body,
  and the life everlasting.
  Amen.

APOSTLES' CREED

HAIL, HOLY QUEEN, MOTHER OF MERCY,

hail, our life, our sweetness, and our hope.
To you we cry, the children of Eve;
  to you we send up our sighs,
mourning and weeping in this land of exile.
Turn, then, most gracious advocate,
  your eyes of mercy toward us;
  lead us home at last
and show us the blessed fruit of your womb,
  Jesus:
O clement, O loving, O sweet Virgin Mary.

HAIL, HOLY QUEEN

WE BELIEVE IN ONE GOD,
THE FATHER, THE ALMIGHTY,

maker of heaven and earth,
of all that is seen and unseen.

We believe in one Lord, Jesus Christ,
the only Son of God,
eternally begotten of the Father,
God from God, Light from Light,
true God from true God,
begotten, not made, one in Being with
the Father.
Through him all things were made.
For us men and for our salvation
he came down from heaven:
by the power of the Holy Spirit
he was born of the Virgin Mary,
and became man.
For our sake he was crucified under
Pontius Pilate;
he suffered, died, and was buried.
On the third day he rose again
in fulfillment of the Scriptures;
he ascended into heaven
and is seated at the right hand of the
Father.
He will come again in glory to judge
the living and the dead,
and his kingdom will have no end.

We believe in the Holy Spirit, the Lord,
the giver of life,
who proceeds from the Father and the
Son.
With the Father and the Son he is
worshiped and glorified.
He has spoken through the Prophets.
We believe in one holy catholic and
apostolic Church.
We acknowledge one baptism for the
forgiveness of sins.
We look for the resurrection of the dead,
and the life of the world to come.
Amen.

NICENE CREED

JOYFUL MYSTERIES

1. The annunciation
2. The visitation
3. The nativity
4. The presentation
5. The finding of Jesus in the Temple

SORROWFUL MYSTERIES

1. The agony in the garden
2. The scourging at the pillar
3. The crowning with thorns
4. The carrying of the cross
5. The crucifixion

GLORIOUS MYSTERIES

1. The resurrection
2. The ascension
3. The coming of the Holy Spirit
4. The assumption of Mary
5. The coronation of Mary

MYSTERIES OF THE ROSARY

OUR FATHER,
WHO ART IN HEAVEN,

hallowed be thy name;
thy kingdom come;
thy will be done on earth as it is
in heaven.
Give us this day our daily bread;
and forgive us our trespasses
as we forgive those who trespass
against us;
and lead us not into temptation,
but deliver us from evil.
Amen.

OUR FATHER

LORD, HAVE MERCY

LORD, HAVE MERCY

Christ, have mercy; Christ, have mercy
Lord, have mercy; Lord, have mercy

(The response to each of the
following is "Pray for us.")

Holy Mary, Mother of God
Saint Augustine
Saint Catherine
Saint Gregory
Saint Ignatius of Antioch
Saint John the Baptist
Saint Joseph
Saint Peter and Saint Paul
Saint Teresa
All holy men and women

SELECTIONS FROM THE LITANY OF SAINTS

MY GOD,

I AM SORRY FOR MY SINS WITH ALL MY HEART.

In choosing to do wrong
and failing to do good,
I have sinned against you
whom I should love above all things.
I firmly intend, with your help,
to do penance,
to sin no more,
and to avoid whatever leads me to sin.
Our Savior Jesus Christ
suffered and died for us.
In his name, my God, have mercy.

ACT OF CONTRITION

THE ANGEL SPOKE

GOD'S MESSAGE TO MARY,

and she conceived of the Holy Spirit.
Hail, Mary. . . .

"I am the lowly servant of the Lord:
let it be done to me according to your word."
Hail, Mary. . . .

And the Word became flesh
and lived among us.
Hail, Mary. . . .

Pray for us, holy Mother of God,
that we may become worthy of the
promises of Christ.

Let us pray.

Lord,
fill our hearts with your grace:
once, through the message of an angel you
revealed to us the incarnation of your Son;
now, through his suffering and death
lead us to the glory of his resurrection.
We ask this through Christ our Lord.
Amen.

THE ANGELUS

ALMIGHTY AND ETERNAL GOD,

YOU GATHER THE SCATTERED SHEEP

and watch over those you have gathered.

Look kindly on all who follow Jesus, your Son.
You have marked them with the seal of
one baptism,
now make them one in the fullness of faith
and unite them in the bond of love.
We ask this through Christ our Lord.
Amen.

PRAYER FOR UNITY

Index

Italicized numbers refer to definitions   **Bold-faced** numbers refer to chapters